United States Court of Appeals

FOR THE DISTRICT OF COLUMBIA CIRCUIT

Argued February 26 and 27, 2001

Decided June 28, 2001

No. 00-5212

United States of America,
Appellee

v.

Microsoft Corporation,
Appellant

Consolidated with
00-5213

Appeals from the United States District Court
for the District of Columbia
(No. 98cv01232)
(No. 98cv01233)

Richard J. Urowsky and Steven L. Holley argued the
causes for appellant. With them on the briefs were John L.

Warden, Richard C. Pepperman, II, William H. Neukom, Thomas W. Burt, David A. Heiner, Jr., Charles F. Rule, Robert A. Long, Jr., and Carter G. Phillips. Christopher J. Meyers entered an appearance.

Lars H. Liebeler, Griffin B. Bell, Lloyd N. Cutler, Louis R. Cohen, C. Boyden Gray, William J. Kolasky, William F. Adkinson, Jr., Jeffrey D. Ayer, and Jay V. Prabhu were on the brief of amici curiae The Association for Competitive Technology and Computing Technology Industry Association in support of appellant.

David R. Burton was on the brief for amicus curiae Center for the Moral Defense of Capitalism in support of appellant.

Robert S. Getman was on the brief for amicus curiae Association for Objective Law in support of appellant.

Jeffrey P. Minear and David C. Frederick, Assistants to the Solicitor General, United States Department of Justice, and John G. Roberts, Jr., argued the causes for appellees. With them on the brief were A. Douglas Melamed, Acting Assistant Attorney General, United States Department of Justice, Jeffrey H. Blattner, Deputy Assistant Attorney General, Catherine G. O'Sullivan, Robert B. Nicholson, Adam D. Hirsh, Andrea Limmer, David Seidman, and Christopher Sprigman, Attorneys, Eliot Spitzer, Attorney General, State of New York, Richard L. Schwartz, Assistant Attorney General, and Kevin J. O'Connor, Office of the Attorney General, State of Wisconsin.

John Rogovin, Kenneth W. Starr, John F. Wood, Elizabeth Petrela, Robert H. Bork, Jason M. Mahler, Stephen M. Shapiro, Donald M. Falk, Mitchell S. Pettit, Kevin J. Arquit, and Michael C. Naughton were on the brief for amici curiae America Online, Inc., et al., in support of appellee. Paul T. Cappuccio entered an appearance.

Lee A. Hollaar, appearing pro se, was on the brief for amicus curiae Lee A. Hollaar.

Carl Lundgren, appearing pro se, was on the brief for amicus curiae Carl Lundgren.

Table of Contents

Before: Edwards, Chief Judge, Williams, Ginsburg,
Sentelle, Randolph, Rogers and Tatel, Circuit Judges.

Opinion for the Court filed Per Curiam.

Per Curiam: Microsoft Corporation appeals from judgments of the District Court finding the company in violation
of ss 1 and 2 of the Sherman Act and ordering various
remedies.

The action against Microsoft arose pursuant to a complaint
filed by the United States and separate complaints filed by
individual States. The District Court determined that Microsoft had maintained a monopoly in the market for Intel-
compatible PC operating systems in violation of s 2; attempted to gain a monopoly in the market for internet browsers in
violation of s 2; and illegally tied two purportedly separate
products, Windows and Internet Explorer ("IE"), in violation
of s 1. United States v. Microsoft Corp., 87 F. Supp. 2d 30
(D.D.C. 2000) ("Conclusions of Law"). The District Court
then found that the same facts that established liability under
ss 1 and 2 of the Sherman Act mandated findings of liability
under analogous state law antitrust provisions. Id. To remedy the Sherman Act violations, the District Court issued a
Final Judgment requiring Microsoft to submit a proposed
plan of divestiture, with the company to be split into an
operating systems business and an applications business.
United States v. Microsoft Corp., 97 F. Supp. 2d 59, 64-65
(D.D.C. 2000) ("Final Judgment"). The District Court's remedial order also contains a number of interim restrictions on
Microsoft's conduct. Id. at 66-69.

Microsoft's appeal contests both the legal conclusions and
the resulting remedial order. There are three principal
aspects of this appeal. First, Microsoft challenges the District Court's legal conclusions as to all three alleged antitrust
violations and also a number of the procedural and factual
foundations on which they rest. Second, Microsoft argues
that the remedial order must be set aside, because the
District Court failed to afford the company an evidentiary
hearing on disputed facts and, also, because the substantive
provisions of the order are flawed. Finally, Microsoft asserts
that the trial judge committed ethical violations by engaging
in impermissible ex parte contacts and making inappropriate

public comments on the merits of the case while it was
pending. Microsoft argues that these ethical violations com-
promised the District Judge's appearance of impartiality,
thereby necessitating his disqualification and vacatur of his
Findings of Fact, Conclusions of Law, and Final Judgment.

After carefully considering the voluminous record on ap-
peal--including the District Court's Findings of Fact and
Conclusions of Law, the testimony and exhibits submitted at
trial, the parties' briefs, and the oral arguments before this
court--we find that some but not all of Microsoft's liability
challenges have merit. Accordingly, we affirm in part and
reverse in part the District Court's judgment that Microsoft
violated s 2 of the Sherman Act by employing anticompetitive
means to maintain a monopoly in the operating system market; we reverse the District Court's determination that Mi-

crosoft violated s 2 of the Sherman Act by illegally attempt-
ing to monopolize the internet browser market; and we
remand the District Court's finding that Microsoft violated
s 1 of the Sherman Act by unlawfully tying its browser to its
operating system. Our judgment extends to the District
Court's findings with respect to the state law counterparts of
the plaintiffs' Sherman Act claims.

We also find merit in Microsoft's challenge to the Final
Judgment embracing the District Court's remedial order.
There are several reasons supporting this conclusion. First,
the District Court's Final Judgment rests on a number of
liability determinations that do not survive appellate review;
therefore, the remedial order as currently fashioned cannot
stand. Furthermore, we would vacate and remand the remedial order even were we to uphold the District Court's
liability determinations in their entirety, because the District
Court failed to hold an evidentiary hearing to address remedies-specific factual disputes.

Finally, we vacate the Final Judgment on remedies, because the trial judge engaged in impermissible ex parte
contacts by holding secret interviews with members of the
media and made numerous offensive comments about Microsoft officials in public statements outside of the courtroom,
giving rise to an appearance of partiality. Although we find
no evidence of actual bias, we hold that the actions of the trial

judge seriously tainted the proceedings before the District
Court and called into question the integrity of the judicial
process. We are therefore constrained to vacate the Final
Judgment on remedies, remand the case for reconsideration
of the remedial order, and require that the case be assigned
to a different trial judge on remand. We believe that this
disposition will be adequate to cure the cited improprieties.

In sum, for reasons more fully explained below, we affirm
in part, reverse in part, and remand in part the District
Court's judgment assessing liability. We vacate in full the
Final Judgment embodying the remedial order and remand
the case to a different trial judge for further proceedings
consistent with this opinion.

I. Introduction

A. Background

In July 1994, officials at the Department of Justice
("DOJ"), on behalf of the United States, filed suit against
Microsoft, charging the company with, among other things,
unlawfully maintaining a monopoly in the operating system
market through anticompetitive terms in its licensing and
software developer agreements. The parties subsequently
entered into a consent decree, thus avoiding a trial on the
merits. See United States v. Microsoft Corp., 56 F.3d 1448
(D.C. Cir. 1995) ("Microsoft I"). Three years later, the
Justice Department filed a civil contempt action against Microsoft for allegedly violating one of the decree's provisions.
On appeal from a grant of a preliminary injunction, this court
held that Microsoft's technological bundling of IE 3.0 and 4.0
with Windows 95 did not violate the relevant provision of the
consent decree. United States v. Microsoft Corp., 147 F.3d
935 (D.C. Cir. 1998) ("Microsoft II"). We expressly reserved
the question whether such bundling might independently
violate ss 1 or 2 of the Sherman Act. Id. at 950 n.14.

On May 18, 1998, shortly before issuance of the Microsoft
II decision, the United States and a group of State plaintiffs

filed separate (and soon thereafter consolidated) complaints, asserting antitrust violations by Microsoft and seeking preliminary and permanent injunctions against the company's allegedly unlawful conduct. The complaints also sought any "other preliminary and permanent relief as is necessary and appropriate to restore competitive conditions in the markets affected by Microsoft's unlawful conduct." Gov't's Compl. at 53, United States v. Microsoft Corp., No. 98-1232 (D.D.C. 1999). Relying almost exclusively on Microsoft's varied efforts to unseat Netscape Navigator as the preeminent internet browser, plaintiffs charged four distinct violations of the Sherman Act: (1) unlawful exclusive dealing arrangements in violation of s 1; (2) unlawful tying of IE to Windows 95 and Windows 98 in violation of s 1; (3) unlawful maintenance of a monopoly in the PC operating system market in violation of s 2; and (4) unlawful attempted monopolization of the internet browser market in violation of s 2. The States also brought pendent claims charging Microsoft with violations of various State antitrust laws.

The District Court scheduled the case on a "fast track." The hearing on the preliminary injunction and the trial on the merits were consolidated pursuant to Fed. R. Civ. P. 65(a)(2). The trial was then scheduled to commence on September 8, 1998, less than four months after the complaints had been filed. In a series of pretrial orders, the District Court limited each side to a maximum of 12 trial witnesses plus two rebuttal witnesses. It required that all trial witnesses' direct testimony be submitted to the court in the form of written declarations. The District Court also made allowances for the use of deposition testimony at trial to prove subordinate or predicate issues. Following the grant of three brief continuances, the trial started on October 19, 1998.

After a 76-day bench trial, the District Court issued its Findings of Fact. United States v. Microsoft Corp., 84 F. Supp. 2d 9 (D.D.C. 1999) ("Findings of Fact"). This triggered two independent courses of action. First, the District Court established a schedule for briefing on possible legal conclusions, inviting Professor Lawrence Lessig to participate as amicus curiae. Second, the District Court re-

ferred the case to mediation to afford the parties an opportunity to settle their differences. The Honorable Richard A.
Posner, Chief Judge of the United States Court of Appeals
for the Seventh Circuit, was appointed to serve as mediator.
The parties concurred in the referral to mediation and in the
choice of mediator.

Mediation failed after nearly four months of settlement
talks between the parties. On April 3, 2000, with the parties'
briefs having been submitted and considered, the District
Court issued its conclusions of law. The District Court found
Microsoft liable on the s 1 tying and s 2 monopoly maintenance and attempted monopolization claims, Conclusions of
Law, at 35-51, while ruling that there was insufficient evidence to support a s 1 exclusive dealing violation, id. at 51-
54. As to the pendent State actions, the District Court found
the State antitrust laws conterminous with ss 1 and 2 of the
Sherman Act, thereby obviating the need for further State-
specific analysis. Id. at 54-56. In those few cases where a
State's law required an additional showing of intrastate impact on competition, the District Court found the requirement
easily satisfied on the evidence at hand. Id. at 55.

Having found Microsoft liable on all but one count, the
District Court then asked plaintiffs to submit a proposed
remedy. Plaintiffs' proposal for a remedial order was subsequently filed within four weeks, along with six supplemental
declarations and over 50 new exhibits. In their proposal,
plaintiffs sought specific conduct remedies, plus structural
relief that would split Microsoft into an applications company
and an operating systems company. The District Court
rejected Microsoft's request for further evidentiary proceedings and, following a single hearing on the merits of the
remedy question, issued its Final Judgment on June 7, 2000.
The District Court adopted plaintiffs' proposed remedy without substantive change.

Microsoft filed a notice of appeal within a week after the
District Court issued its Final Judgment. This court then
ordered that any proceedings before it be heard by the court
sitting en banc. Before any substantive matters were ad-

dressed by this court, however, the District Court certified
appeal of the case brought by the United States directly to
the Supreme Court pursuant to 15 U.S.C. s 29(b), while
staying the final judgment order in the federal and state
cases pending appeal. The States thereafter petitioned the
Supreme Court for a writ of certiorari in their case. The
Supreme Court declined to hear the appeal of the Government's case and remanded the matter to this court; the Court
likewise denied the States' petition for writ of certiorari.
Microsoft Corp. v. United States, 530 U.S. 1301 (2000). This
consolidated appeal followed.

B.   Overview

     Before turning to the merits of Microsoft's various argu-
ments, we pause to reflect briefly on two matters of note, one
practical and one theoretical.

     The practical matter relates to the temporal dimension of
this case. The litigation timeline in this case is hardly
problematic. Indeed, it is noteworthy that a case of this
magnitude and complexity has proceeded from the filing of
complaints through trial to appellate decision in a mere three
years. See, e.g., Data Gen. Corp. v. Grumman Sys. Support
Corp., 36 F.3d 1147, 1155 (1st Cir. 1994) (six years from filing
of complaint to appellate decision); Transamerica Computer
Co., Inc. v. IBM, 698 F.2d 1377, 1381 (9th Cir. 1983) (over
four years from start of trial to appellate decision); United
States v. United Shoe Mach. Corp., 110 F. Supp. 295, 298 (D.
Mass. 1953) (over five years from filing of complaint to trial
court decision).

     What is somewhat problematic, however, is that just over
six years have passed since Microsoft engaged in the first
conduct plaintiffs allege to be anticompetitive. As the record
in this case indicates, six years seems like an eternity in the
computer industry. By the time a court can assess liability,
firms, products, and the marketplace are likely to have
changed dramatically. This, in turn, threatens enormous
practical difficulties for courts considering the appropriate
measure of relief in equitable enforcement actions, both in
crafting injunctive remedies in the first instance and review-

ing those remedies in the second. Conduct remedies may be
unavailing in such cases, because innovation to a large degree
has already rendered the anticompetitive conduct obsolete
(although by no means harmless). And broader structural
remedies present their own set of problems, including how a
court goes about restoring competition to a dramatically
changed, and constantly changing, marketplace. That is just
one reason why we find the District Court's refusal in the
present case to hold an evidentiary hearing on remedies--to
update and flesh out the available information before seriously entertaining the possibility of dramatic structural relief--so
problematic. See infra Section V.

    We do not mean to say that enforcement actions will no
longer play an important role in curbing infringements of the
antitrust laws in technologically dynamic markets, nor do we
assume this in assessing the merits of this case. Even in
those cases where forward-looking remedies appear limited,
the Government will continue to have an interest in defining
the contours of the antitrust laws so that law-abiding firms
will have a clear sense of what is permissible and what is not.
And the threat of private damage actions will remain to deter
those firms inclined to test the limits of the law.

    The second matter of note is more theoretical in nature.
We decide this case against a backdrop of significant debate
amongst academics and practitioners over the extent to
which "old economy" s 2 monopolization doctrines should
apply to firms competing in dynamic technological markets
characterized by network effects. In markets characterized
by network effects, one product or standard tends towards
dominance, because "the utility that a user derives from con-
sumption of the good increases with the number of other
agents consuming the good." Michael L. Katz & Carl Shapiro, Network Externalities, Competition, and Compatibility,
75 Am. Econ. Rev. 424, 424 (1985). For example, "[a]n
individual consumer's demand to use (and hence her benefit
from) the telephone network ... increases with the number
of other users on the network whom she can call or from
whom she can receive calls." Howard A. Shelanski & J.
Gregory Sidak, Antitrust Divestiture in Network Industries,

68 U. Chi. L. Rev. 1, 8 (2001). Once a product or standard achieves wide acceptance, it becomes more or less entrenched. Competition in such industries is "for the field" rather than "within the field." See Harold Demsetz, Why Regulate Utilities?, 11 J.L. & Econ. 55, 57 & n.7 (1968) (emphasis omitted).

In technologically dynamic markets, however, such entrenchment may be temporary, because innovation may alter the field altogether. See Joseph A. Schumpeter, Capitalism, Socialism and Democracy 81-90 (Harper Perennial 1976) (1942). Rapid technological change leads to markets in which "firms compete through innovation for temporary market dominance, from which they may be displaced by the next wave of product advancements." Shelanski & Sidak, at 11-12 (discussing Schumpeterian competition, which proceeds "sequentially over time rather than simultaneously across a market"). Microsoft argues that the operating system market is just such a market.

Whether or not Microsoft's characterization of the operating system market is correct does not appreciably alter our mission in assessing the alleged antitrust violations in the present case. As an initial matter, we note that there is no consensus among commentators on the question of whether, and to what extent, current monopolization doctrine should be amended to account for competition in technologically dynamic markets characterized by network effects. Compare Steven C. Salop & R. Craig Romaine, Preserving Monopoly: Economic Analysis, Legal Standards, and Microsoft, 7 Geo. Mason L. Rev. 617, 654-55, 663-64 (1999) (arguing that exclusionary conduct in high-tech networked industries deserves heightened antitrust scrutiny in part because it may threaten to deter innovation), with Ronald A. Cass & Keith N. Hylton, Preserving Competition: Economic Analysis, Legal Standards and Microsoft, 8 Geo. Mason L. Rev. 1, 36-39 (1999) (equivocating on the antitrust implications of network effects and noting that the presence of network externalities may actually encourage innovation by guaranteeing more durable monopolies to innovating winners). Indeed, there is some suggestion that the economic consequences of network effects and technological dynamism act to offset one another, thereby making it difficult to formulate categorical antitrust rules absent a particularized analysis of a given market. See Shelanski & Sidak, at 6-7 ("High profit margins might appear to be the benign and necessary recovery of legitimate investment returns in a Schumpeterian framework, but they might represent exploitation of customer lock-in and monopoly power when viewed through the lens of network economics.... The issue is particularly complex because, in network industries characterized by rapid innovation, both forces may be operating and can be difficult to isolate.").

Moreover, it should be clear that Microsoft makes no claim that anticompetitive conduct should be assessed differently in technologically dynamic markets. It claims only that the measure of monopoly power should be different. For reasons fully discussed below, we reject Microsoft's monopoly power argument. See infra Section II.A.

With this backdrop in mind, we turn to the specific challenges raised in Microsoft's appeal.

II. Monopolization

Section 2 of the Sherman Act makes it unlawful for a firm to "monopolize." 15 U.S.C. s 2. The offense of monopolization has two elements: "(1) the possession of monopoly power in the relevant market and (2) the willful acquisition or maintenance of that power as distinguished from growth or development as a consequence of a superior product, business acumen, or historic accident." United States v. Grinnell Corp., 384 U.S. 563, 570-71 (1966). The District Court applied this test and found that Microsoft possesses monopoly power in the market for Intel-compatible PC operating systems. Focusing primarily on Microsoft's efforts to suppress Netscape Navigator's threat to its operating system monopoly, the court also found that Microsoft maintained its power not through competition on the merits, but through unlawful means. Microsoft challenges both conclusions. We defer to the District Court's findings of fact, setting them aside only if clearly erroneous. Fed R. Civ. P. 52(a). We review legal

questions de novo. United States ex rel. Modern Elec., Inc.
v. Ideal Elec. Sec. Co., 81 F.3d 240, 244 (D.C. Cir. 1996).

We begin by considering whether Microsoft possesses monopoly power, see infra Section II.A, and finding that it does,
we turn to the question whether it maintained this power
through anticompetitive means. Agreeing with the District
Court that the company behaved anticompetitively, see infra
Section II.B, and that these actions contributed to the maintenance of its monopoly power, see infra Section II.C, we affirm
the court's finding of liability for monopolization.

A.   Monopoly Power

While merely possessing monopoly power is not itself an
antitrust violation, see Northeastern Tel. Co. v. AT & T, 651
F.2d 76, 84-85 (2d Cir. 1981), it is a necessary element of a
monopolization charge, see Grinnell, 384 U.S. at 570. The
Supreme Court defines monopoly power as "the power to
control prices or exclude competition." United States v. E.I.
du Pont de Nemours & Co., 351 U.S. 377, 391 (1956). More
precisely, a firm is a monopolist if it can profitably raise
prices substantially above the competitive level. 2A Phillip
E. Areeda et al., Antitrust Law p 501, at 85 (1995); cf. Ball
Mem'l Hosp., Inc. v. Mut. Hosp. Ins., Inc., 784 F.2d 1325,
1335 (7th Cir. 1986) (defining market power as "the ability to
cut back the market's total output and so raise price").
Where evidence indicates that a firm has in fact profitably
done so, the existence of monopoly power is clear. See Rebel
Oil Co. v. Atl. Richfield Co., 51 F.3d 1421, 1434 (9th Cir.
1995); see also FTC v. Indiana Fed'n of Dentists, 476 U.S.
447, 460-61 (1986) (using direct proof to show market power
in Sherman Act s 1 unreasonable restraint of trade action).
Because such direct proof is only rarely available, courts
more typically examine market structure in search of circumstantial evidence of monopoly power. 2A Areeda et al.,
Antitrust Law p 531a, at 156; see also, e.g., Grinnell, 384 U.S.
at 571. Under this structural approach, monopoly power may
be inferred from a firm's possession of a dominant share of a
relevant market that is protected by entry barriers. See

Rebel Oil, 51 F.3d at 1434. "Entry barriers" are factors
(such as certain regulatory requirements) that prevent new
rivals from timely responding to an increase in price above
the competitive level. See S. Pac. Communications Co. v.
AT & T, 740 F.2d 980, 1001-02 (D.C. Cir. 1984).

The District Court considered these structural factors and
concluded that Microsoft possesses monopoly power in a
relevant market. Defining the market as Intel-compatible
PC operating systems, the District Court found that Microsoft has a greater than 95% share. It also found the company's market position protected by a substantial entry barrier.
Conclusions of Law, at 36.

Microsoft argues that the District Court incorrectly defined
the relevant market. It also claims that there is no barrier to
entry in that market. Alternatively, Microsoft argues that
because the software industry is uniquely dynamic, direct
proof, rather than circumstantial evidence, more appropriate-
ly indicates whether it possesses monopoly power. Rejecting
each argument, we uphold the District Court's finding of
monopoly power in its entirety.

1. Market Structure

a. Market definition

"Because the ability of consumers to turn to other suppliers
restrains a firm from raising prices above the competitive
level," Rothery Storage & Van Co. v. Atlas Van Lines, Inc.,
792 F.2d 210, 218 (D.C. Cir. 1986), the relevant market must
include all products "reasonably interchangeable by consumers for the same purposes." du Pont, 351 U.S. at 395. In
this case, the District Court defined the market as "the
licensing of all Intel-compatible PC operating systems worldwide," finding that there are "currently no products--and ...
there are not likely to be any in the near future--that a
significant percentage of computer users worldwide could
substitute for [these operating systems] without incurring
substantial costs." Conclusions of Law, at 36. Calling this
market definition "far too narrow," Appellant's Opening Br.
at 84, Microsoft argues that the District Court improperly

excluded three types of products: non-Intel compatible operating systems (primarily Apple's Macintosh operating system,
Mac OS), operating systems for non-PC devices (such as
handheld computers and portal websites), and "middleware"
products, which are not operating systems at all.

We begin with Mac OS. Microsoft's argument that Mac
OS should have been included in the relevant market suffers
from a flaw that infects many of the company's monopoly
power claims: the company fails to challenge the District
Court's factual findings, or to argue that these findings do not
support the court's conclusions. The District Court found
that consumers would not switch from Windows to Mac OS in
response to a substantial price increase because of the costs
of acquiring the new hardware needed to run Mac OS (an
Apple computer and peripherals) and compatible software
applications, as well as because of the effort involved in
learning the new system and transferring files to its format.
Findings of Fact p 20. The court also found the Apple
system less appealing to consumers because it costs consider-
ably more and supports fewer applications. Id. p 21. Microsoft responds only by saying: "the district court's market
definition is so narrow that it excludes Apple's Mac OS, which
has competed with Windows for years, simply because the
Mac OS runs on a different microprocessor." Appellant's
Opening Br. at 84. This general, conclusory statement falls
far short of what is required to challenge findings as clearly
erroneous. Pendleton v. Rumsfeld, 628 F.2d 102, 106 (D.C.
Cir. 1980); see also Terry v. Reno, 101 F.3d 1412, 1415 (D.C.
Cir. 1996) (holding that claims made but not argued in a brief
are waived). Microsoft neither points to evidence contradict-
ing the District Court's findings nor alleges that supporting
record evidence is insufficient. And since Microsoft does not
argue that even if we accept these findings, they do not
support the District Court's conclusion, we have no basis for
upsetting the court's decision to exclude Mac OS from the
relevant market.

Microsoft's challenge to the District Court's exclusion of
non-PC based competitors, such as information appliances
(handheld devices, etc.) and portal websites that host server-
based software applications, suffers from the same defect:

the company fails to challenge the District Court's key factual findings. In particular, the District Court found that because information appliances fall far short of performing all of the functions of a PC, most consumers will buy them only as a supplement to their PCs. Findings of Fact p 23. The District Court also found that portal websites do not presently host enough applications to induce consumers to switch, nor are they likely to do so in the near future. Id. p 27. Again, because Microsoft does not argue that the District Court's findings do not support its conclusion that information appliances and portal websites are outside the relevant market, we adhere to that conclusion.

This brings us to Microsoft's main challenge to the District Court's market definition: the exclusion of middleware. Because of the importance of middleware to this case, we pause to explain what it is and how it relates to the issue before us.

Operating systems perform many functions, including allocating computer memory and controlling peripherals such as printers and keyboards. See Direct Testimony of Frederick Warren-Boulton p 20, reprinted in 5 J.A. at 3172-73. Operating systems also function as platforms for software applications. They do this by "exposing"--i.e., making available to software developers--routines or protocols that perform certain widely-used functions. These are known as Application Programming Interfaces, or "APIs." See Direct Testimony of James Barksdale p 70, reprinted in 5 J.A. at 2895-96. For example, Windows contains an API that enables users to draw a box on the screen. See Direct Testimony of Michael T. Devlin p 12, reprinted in 5 J.A. at 3525. Software developers wishing to include that function in an application need not duplicate it in their own code. Instead, they can "call"--i.e., use--the Windows API. See Direct Testimony of James Barksdale p p 70-71, reprinted in 5 J.A. at 2895-97. Windows contains thousands of APIs, controlling everything from data storage to font display. See Direct Testimony of Michael Devlin p 12, reprinted in 5 J.A. at 3525.

Every operating system has different APIs. Accordingly, a developer who writes an application for one operating system and wishes to sell the application to users of another must modify, or "port," the application to the second operating system. Findings of Fact p 4. This process is both time-consuming and expensive. Id. p 30.

"Middleware" refers to software products that expose their own APIs. Id. p 28; Direct Testimony of Paul Maritz p p 234-36, reprinted in 6 J.A. at 3727-29. Because of this, a middleware product written for Windows could take over some or all of Windows's valuable platform functions--that is, developers might begin to rely upon APIs exposed by the middleware for basic routines rather than relying upon the API set included in Windows. If middleware were written for multiple operating systems, its impact could be even greater. The more developers could rely upon APIs exposed by such middleware, the less expensive porting to different operating systems would be. Ultimately, if developers could write applications relying exclusively on APIs exposed by middleware, their applications would run on any operating system on which the middleware was also present. See Direct Testimony of Avadis Tevanian, Jr. p 45, reprinted in 5 J.A. at 3113. Netscape Navigator and Java--both at issue in this case--are middleware products written for multiple operating systems. Findings of Fact p 28.

Microsoft argues that, because middleware could usurp the operating system's platform function and might eventually take over other operating system functions (for instance, by controlling peripherals), the District Court erred in excluding Navigator and Java from the relevant market. The District Court found, however, that neither Navigator, Java, nor any other middleware product could now, or would soon, expose enough APIs to serve as a platform for popular applications, much less take over all operating system functions. Id. p p 28-29. Again, Microsoft fails to challenge these findings, instead simply asserting middleware's "potential" as a competitor. Appellant's Opening Br. at 86. The test of reasonable interchangeability, however, required the District Court to consider only substitutes that constrain pricing in the reasonably foreseeable future, and only products that can enter the market in a relatively short time can perform this function. See Rothery, 792 F.2d at 218 ("Because the ability

of consumers to turn to other suppliers restrains a firm from
raising prices above the competitive level, the definition of the
'relevant market' rests on a determination of available substitutes."); see also Findings of Fact p 29 ("[I]t would take
several years for middleware ... to evolve" into a product
that can constrain operating system pricing.). Whatever
middleware's ultimate potential, the District Court found that
consumers could not now abandon their operating systems
and switch to middleware in response to a sustained price for
Windows above the competative level. Findings of Fact
p p 28, 29. Nor is middleware likely to overtake the operating system as the primary platform for software development
any time in the near future. Id.

    Alternatively, Microsoft argues that the District Court
should not have excluded middleware from the relevant market because the primary focus of the plaintiffs' s 2 charge is
on Microsoft's attempts to suppress middleware's threat to its
operating system monopoly. According to Microsoft, it is
"contradict[ory]," 2/26/2001 Ct. Appeals Tr. at 20, to define
the relevant market to exclude the "very competitive threats
that gave rise" to the action. Appellant's Opening Br. at 84.
The purported contradiction lies between plaintiffs' s 2 theory, under which Microsoft preserved its monopoly against
middleware technologies that threatened to become viable
substitutes for Windows, and its theory of the relevant market, under which middleware is not presently a viable substitute for Windows. Because middleware's threat is only nascent, however, no contradiction exists. Nothing in s 2 of the
Sherman Act limits its prohibition to actions taken against
threats that are already well-developed enough to serve as
present substitutes. See infra Section II.C. Because market
definition is meant to identify products "reasonably interchangeable by consumers," du Pont, 351 U.S. at 395, and
because middleware is not now interchangeable with Windows, the District Court had good reason for excluding
middleware from the relevant market.

    b. Market power

    Having thus properly defined the relevant market, the
District Court found that Windows accounts for a greater
than 95% share. Findings of Fact p 35. The court also

found that even if Mac OS were included, Microsoft's share would exceed 80%. Id. Microsoft challenges neither finding, nor does it argue that such a market share is not predominant. Cf. Grinnell, 384 U.S. at 571 (87% is predominant); Eastman Kodak Co. v. Image Technical Servs., Inc., 504 U.S. 451, 481 (1992) (80%); du Pont, 351 U.S. at 379, 391 (75%).

Instead, Microsoft claims that even a predominant market share does not by itself indicate monopoly power. Although the "existence of [monopoly] power ordinarily may be inferred from the predominant share of the market," Grinnell, 384 U.S. at 571, we agree with Microsoft that because of the possibility of competition from new entrants, see Ball Mem'l Hosp., Inc., 784 F.2d at 1336, looking to current market share alone can be "misleading." Hunt-Wesson Foods, Inc. v. Ragu Foods, Inc., 627 F.2d 919, 924 (9th Cir. 1980); see also Ball Mem'l Hosp., Inc., 784 F.2d at 1336 ("Market share reflects current sales, but today's sales do not always indicate power over sales and price tomorrow.") In this case, however, the District Court was not misled. Considering the possibility of new rivals, the court focused not only on Microsoft's present market share, but also on the structural barrier that protects the company's future position. Conclusions of Law, at 36. That barrier--the "applications barrier to entry"--stems from two characteristics of the software market: (1) most consumers prefer operating systems for which a large number of applications have already been written; and (2) most developers prefer to write for operating systems that already have a substantial consumer base. See Findings of Fact p p 30, 36. This "chicken-and-egg" situation ensures that applications will continue to be written for the already dominant Windows, which in turn ensures that consumers will continue to prefer it over other operating systems. Id.

Challenging the existence of the applications barrier to entry, Microsoft observes that software developers do write applications for other operating systems, pointing out that at its peak IBM's OS/2 supported approximately 2,500 applications. Id. p 46. This misses the point. That some developers write applications for other operating systems is not at all inconsistent with the finding that the applications barrier to entry discourages many from writing for these less popular platforms. Indeed, the District Court found that IBM's difficulty in attracting a larger number of software developers to write for its platform seriously impeded OS/2's success. Id. p 46.

Microsoft does not dispute that Windows supports many more applications than any other operating system. It argues instead that "[i]t defies common sense" to suggest that an operating system must support as many applications as Windows does (more than 70,000, according to the District Court, id. p 40) to be competitive. Appellant's Opening Br. at 96. Consumers, Microsoft points out, can only use a very small percentage of these applications. Id. As the District Court explained, however, the applications barrier to entry gives consumers reason to prefer the dominant operating system even if they have no need to use all applications written for it:

> The consumer wants an operating system that runs not only types of applications that he knows he will want to use, but also those types in which he might develop an interest later. Also, the consumer knows that if he chooses an operating system with enough demand to support multiple applications in each product category, he will be less likely to find himself straitened later by having to use an application whose features disappoint him. Finally, the average user knows that, generally speaking, applications improve through successive versions. He thus wants an operating system for which successive generations of his favorite applications will be released--promptly at that. The fact that a vastly larger number of applications are written for Windows than for other PC operating systems attracts consumers to Windows, because it reassures them that their interests will be met as long as they use Microsoft's product.

Findings of Fact p 37. Thus, despite the limited success of its rivals, Microsoft benefits from the applications barrier to entry.

Of course, were middleware to succeed, it would erode the applications barrier to entry. Because applications written for multiple operating systems could run on any operating system on which the middleware product was present with little, if any, porting, the operating system market would become competitive. Id. p p 29, 72. But as the District Court found, middleware will not expose a sufficient number of APIs to erode the applications barrier to entry in the foreseeable future. See id. p p 28-29.

Microsoft next argues that the applications barrier to entry is not an entry barrier at all, but a reflection of Windows' popularity. It is certainly true that Windows may have gained its initial dominance in the operating system market competitively--through superior foresight or quality. But this case is not about Microsoft's initial acquisition of monopoly power. It is about Microsoft's efforts to maintain this position through means other than competition on the merits. Because the applications barrier to entry protects a dominant operating system irrespective of quality, it gives Microsoft power to stave off even superior new rivals. The barrier is thus a characteristic of the operating system market, not of Microsoft's popularity, or, as asserted by a Microsoft witness, the company's efficiency. See Direct Testimony of Richard Schmalensee p 115, reprinted in 25 J.A. at 16153-14.

Finally, Microsoft argues that the District Court should not have considered the applications barrier to entry because it reflects not a cost borne disproportionately by new entrants, but one borne by all participants in the operating system market. According to Microsoft, it had to make major investments to convince software developers to write for its new operating system, and it continues to "evangelize" the Windows platform today. Whether costs borne by all market participants should be considered entry barriers is the subject of much debate. Compare 2A Areeda & Hovenkamp, Antitrust Law s 420c, at 61 (arguing that these costs are entry barriers), and Joe S. Bain, Barriers to New Competition: Their Character and Consequences in Manufacturing Industries 6-7 (1956) (considering these costs entry barriers), with L.A. Land Co. v. Brunswick Corp., 6 F.3d 1422, 1428 (9th Cir. 1993) (evaluating cost based on "[t]he disadvantage of new entrants as compared to incumbents"), and George Stigler, The Organization of Industry 67 (1968) (excluding these costs). We need not resolve this issue, however, for even under the more narrow definition it is clear that there are barriers. When Microsoft entered the operating system market with MS-DOS and the first version of Windows, it did not confront a dominant rival operating system with as massive an installed base and as vast an existing array of applications as the Windows operating systems have since enjoyed. Findings of Fact p p 6, 7, 43. Moreover, when Microsoft introduced Windows 95 and 98, it was able to bypass the applications barrier to entry that protected the incumbent Windows by including APIs from the earlier version in the new operating systems. See id. p 44. This made porting existing Windows applications to the new version of Windows much less costly than porting them to the operating systems of other entrants who could not freely include APIs from the incumbent Windows with their own.

2. Direct Proof

Having sustained the District Court's conclusion that circumstantial evidence proves that Microsoft possesses monopoly power, we turn to Microsoft's alternative argument that it does not behave like a monopolist. Claiming that software competition is uniquely "dynamic," Appellant's Opening Br. at 84 (quoting Findings of Fact p 59), the company suggests a new rule: that monopoly power in the software industry should be proven directly, that is, by examining a company's actual behavior to determine if it reveals the existence of monopoly power. According to Microsoft, not only does no such proof of its power exist, but record evidence demonstrates the absence of monopoly power. The company claims that it invests heavily in research and development, id. at 88-89 (citing Direct Testimony of Paul Maritz p 155, reprinted in 6 J.A. at 3698 (testifying that Microsoft invests approximately 17% of its revenue in R&D)), and charges a low price for Windows (a small percentage of the price of an Intel-compatible PC system and less than the price of its rivals, id. at 90 (citing Findings of Fact p p 19, 21, 46)).

Microsoft's argument fails because, even assuming that the software market is uniquely dynamic in the long term, the District Court correctly applied the structural approach to determine if the company faces competition in the short term.

Structural market power analyses are meant to determine
whether potential substitutes constrain a firm's ability to
raise prices above the competitive level; only threats that are
likely to materialize in the relatively near future perform this
function to any significant degree. Rothery, 792 F.2d at 218
(quoting Lawrence Sullivan, Antitrust s 12, at 41 (1977))
(only substitutes that can enter the market "promptly" should
be considered). The District Court expressly considered and
rejected Microsoft's claims that innovations such as handheld
devices and portal websites would soon expand the relevant
market beyond Intel-compatible PC operating systems. Because the company does not challenge these findings, we have
no reason to believe that prompt substitutes are available.
The structural approach, as applied by the District Court, is
thus capable of fulfilling its purpose even in a changing
market. Microsoft cites no case, nor are we aware of one,
requiring direct evidence to show monopoly power in any
market. We decline to adopt such a rule now.

Even if we were to require direct proof, moreover, Microsoft's behavior may well be sufficient to show the existence of
monopoly power. Certainly, none of the conduct Microsoft
points to--its investment in R&D and the relatively low price
of Windows--is inconsistent with the possession of such power. Conclusions of Law, at 37. The R&D expenditures
Microsoft points to are not simply for Windows, but for its
entire company, which most likely does not possess a monopoly for all of its products. Moreover, because innovation can
increase an already dominant market share and further delay
the emergence of competition, even monopolists have reason
to invest in R&D. Findings of Fact p 61. Microsoft's pricing
behavior is similarly equivocal. The company claims only
that it never charged the short-term profit-maximizing price
for Windows. Faced with conflicting expert testimony, the
District Court found that it could not accurately determine
what this price would be. Id. p 65. In any event, the court
found, a price lower than the short-term profit-maximizing
price is not inconsistent with possession or improper use of
monopoly power. Id. p p 65-66. Cf. Berkey Photo, Inc. v.

Eastman Kodak Co., 603 F.2d 263, 274 (2d Cir. 1979) ("[I]f monopoly power has been acquired or maintained through improper means, the fact that the power has not been used to extract [a monopoly price] provides no succor to the monopolist."). Microsoft never claims that it did not charge the long-term monopoly price. Micosoft does argue that the price of Windows is a fraction of the price of an Intel-compatible PC system and lower than that of rival operating systems, but these facts are not inconsistent with the District Court's finding that Microsoft has monopoly power. See Findings of Fact p 36 ("Intel-compatible PC operating systems other than Windows [would not] attract[ ] significant demand ... even if Micosoft held its prices substantially above the competitive level.").

More telling, the District Court found that some aspects of Microsoft's behavior are difficult to explain unless Windows is a monopoly product. For instance, according to the District Court, the company set the price of Windows without considering rivals' prices, Findings of Fact p 62, something a firm without a monopoly would have been unable to do. The District Court also found that Microsoft's pattern of exclusionary conduct could only be rational "if the firm knew that it possessed monopoly power." Conclusions of Law, at 37. It is to that conduct that we now turn.

B.   Anticompetitive Conduct
    As discussed above, having a monopoly does not by itself violate s 2. A firm violates s 2 only when it acquires or maintains, or attempts to acquire or maintain, a monopoly by engaging in exclusionary conduct "as distinguished from growth or development as a consequence of a superior product, business acumen, or historic accident." Grinnell, 384 U.S. at 571; see also United States v. Aluminum Co. of Am., 148 F.2d 416, 430 (2d Cir. 1945) (Hand, J.) ("The successful competitor, having been urged to compete, must not be turned upon when he wins.").

In this case, after concluding that Microsoft had monopoly power, the District Court held that Microsoft had violated s 2 by engaging in a variety of exclusionary acts (not including predatory pricing), to maintain its monopoly by preventing the effective distribution and use of products that might threaten that monopoly. Specifically, the District Court held Microsoft liable for: (1) the way in which it integrated IE into

Windows; (2) its various dealings with Original Equipment Manufacturers ("OEMs"), Internet Access Providers ("IAPs"), Internet Content Providers ("ICPs"), Independent Software Vendors ("ISVs"), and Apple Computer; (3) its efforts to contain and to subvert Java technologies; and (4) its course of conduct as a whole. Upon appeal, Microsoft argues that it did not engage in any exclusionary conduct.

Whether any particular act of a monopolist is exclusionary, rather than merely a form of vigorous competition, can be difficult to discern: the means of illicit exclusion, like the means of legitimate competition, are myriad. The challenge for an antitrust court lies in stating a general rule for distinguishing between exclusionary acts, which reduce social welfare, and competitive acts, which increase it.

From a century of case law on monopolization under s 2, however, several principles do emerge. First, to be condemned as exclusionary, a monopolist's act must have an "anticompetitive effect." That is, it must harm the competitive process and thereby harm consumers. In contrast, harm to one or more competitors will not suffice. "The [Sherman Act] directs itself not against conduct which is competitive, even severely so, but against conduct which unfairly tends to destroy competition itself." Spectrum Sports, Inc. v. McQuillan, 506 U.S. 447, 458 (1993); see also Brooke Group Ltd. v. Brown & Williamson Tobacco Corp., 509 U.S. 209, 225 (1993) ("Even an act of pure malice by one business competitor against another does not, without more, state a claim under the federal antitrust laws....").

Second, the plaintiff, on whom the burden of proof of course rests, see, e.g., Monsanto Co. v. Spray-Rite Serv. Corp., 465 U.S. 752, 763 (1984); see also United States v. Arnold, Schwinn & Co., 388 U.S. 365, 374 n.5 (1967), overruled on other grounds, Cont'l T.V., Inc. v. GTE Sylvania Inc., 433 U.S. 36 (1977), must demonstrate that the monopolist's conduct indeed has the requisite anticompetitive effect. See generally Brooke Group, 509 U.S. at 225-26. In a case brought by a private plaintiff, the plaintiff must show that its injury is "of 'the type that the statute was intended to

forestall,' " Brunswick Corp. v. Pueblo Bowl-O-Mat, Inc., 429
U.S. 477, 487-88 (1977) (quoting Wyandotte Transp. v. United
States, 389 U.S. 191, 202 (1967)); no less in a case brought by
the Government, it must demonstrate that the monopolist's
conduct harmed competition, not just a competitor.

      Third, if a plaintiff successfully establishes a prima facie
case under s 2 by demonstrating anticompetitive effect, then
the monopolist may proffer a "procompetitive justification"
for its conduct. See Eastman Kodak, 504 U.S. at 483. If the
monopolist asserts a procompetitive justification--a nonpre-
textual claim that its conduct is indeed a form of competition
on the merits because it involves, for example, greater efficiency or enhanced consumer appeal--then the burden shifts
back to the plaintiff to rebut that claim. Cf. Capital Imaging
Assocs., P.C. v. Mohawk Valley Med. Assocs., Inc., 996 F.2d
537, 543 (2d Cir. 1993).

      Fourth, if the monopolist's procompetitive justification
stands unrebutted, then the plaintiff must demonstrate that
the anticompetitive harm of the conduct outweighs the procompetitive benefit. In cases arising under s 1 of the Sherman Act, the courts routinely apply a similar balancing
approach under the rubric of the "rule of reason." The
source of the rule of reason is Standard Oil Co. v. United
States, 221 U.S. 1 (1911), in which the Supreme Court used
that term to describe the proper inquiry under both sections
of the Act. See id. at 61-62 ("[W]hen the second section [of
the Sherman Act] is thus harmonized with ... the first, it
becomes obvious that the criteria to be resorted to in any
given case for the purpose of ascertaining whether violations
of the section have been committed, is the rule of reason
guided by the established law...."). As the Fifth Circuit
more recently explained, "[i]t is clear ... that the analysis
under section 2 is similar to that under section 1 regardless
whether the rule of reason label is applied...." Mid-Texas
Communications Sys., Inc. v. AT & T, 615 F.2d 1372, 1389
n.13 (5th Cir. 1980) (citing Byars v. Bluff City News Co., 609
F.2d 843, 860 (6th Cir. 1979)); see also Cal. Computer Prods.,
Inc. v. IBM Corp., 613 F.2d 727, 737 (9th Cir. 1979).

Finally, in considering whether the monopolist's conduct on balance harms competition and is therefore condemned as exclusionary for purposes of s 2, our focus is upon the effect of that conduct, not upon the intent behind it. Evidence of the intent behind the conduct of a monopolist is relevant only to the extent it helps us understand the likely effect of the monopolist's conduct. See, e.g., Chicago Bd. of Trade v. United States, 246 U.S. 231, 238 (1918) ("knowledge of intent may help the court to interpret facts and to predict consequences"); Aspen Skiing Co. v. Aspen Highlands Skiing Corp., 472 U.S. 585, 603 (1985).

With these principles in mind, we now consider Microsoft's objections to the District Court's holding that Microsoft violated s 2 of the Sherman Act in a variety of ways.

1. Licenses Issued to Original Equipment Manufacturers

The District Court condemned a number of provisions in Microsoft's agreements licensing Windows to OEMs, because it found that Microsoft's imposition of those provisions (like many of Microsoft's other actions at issue in this case) serves to reduce usage share of Netscape's browser and, hence, protect Microsoft's operating system monopoly. The reason market share in the browser market affects market power in the operating system market is complex, and warrants some explanation.

Browser usage share is important because, as we explained in Section II.A above, a browser (or any middleware product, for that matter) must have a critical mass of users in order to attract software developers to write applications relying upon the APIs it exposes, and away from the APIs exposed by Windows. Applications written to a particular browser's APIs, however, would run on any computer with that browser, regardless of the underlying operating system. "The overwhelming majority of consumers will only use a PC operating system for which there already exists a large and varied set of ... applications, and for which it seems relatively certain that new types of applications and new versions of existing applications will continue to be marketed...."

Findings of Fact p 30. If a consumer could have access to the applications he desired--regardless of the operating system he uses--simply by installing a particular browser on his computer, then he would no longer feel compelled to select Windows in order to have access to those applications; he could select an operating system other than Windows based solely upon its quality and price. In other words, the market for operating systems would be competitive.

Therefore, Microsoft's efforts to gain market share in one market (browsers) served to meet the threat to Microsoft's monopoly in another market (operating systems) by keeping rival browsers from gaining the critical mass of users necessary to attract developer attention away from Windows as the platform for software development. Plaintiffs also argue that Microsoft's actions injured competition in the browser market--an argument we will examine below in relation to their specific claims that Microsoft attempted to monopolize the browser market and unlawfully tied its browser to its operating system so as to foreclose competition in the browser market. In evaluating the s 2 monopoly maintenance claim, however, our immediate concern is with the anticompetitive effect of Microsoft's conduct in preserving its monopoly in the operating system market.

In evaluating the restrictions in Microsoft's agreements licensing Windows to OEMs, we first consider whether plaintiffs have made out a prima facie case by demonstrating that the restrictions have an anticompetitive effect. In the next subsection, we conclude that plaintiffs have met this burden as to all the restrictions. We then consider Microsoft's proffered justifications for the restrictions and, for the most part, hold those justifications insufficient.

a. Anticompetitive effect of the license restrictions

The restrictions Microsoft places upon Original Equipment Manufacturers are of particular importance in determining browser usage share because having an OEM pre-install a browser on a computer is one of the two most cost-effective methods by far of distributing browsing software. (The other is bundling the browser with internet access software distrib-

uted by an IAP.) Findings of Fact p 145. The District
Court found that the restrictions Microsoft imposed in licensing Windows to OEMs prevented many OEMs from distributing browsers other than IE. Conclusions of Law, at 39-40.
In particular, the District Court condemned the license provisions prohibiting the OEMs from: (1) removing any desktop
icons, folders, or "Start" menu entries; (2) altering the initial
boot sequence; and (3) otherwise altering the appearance of
the Windows desktop. Findings of Fact p 213.

     The District Court concluded that the first license restric-
tion--the prohibition upon the removal of desktop icons,
folders, and Start menu entries--thwarts the distribution of a
rival browser by preventing OEMs from removing visible
means of user access to IE. Id. p 203. The OEMs cannot
practically install a second browser in addition to IE, the
court found, in part because "[p]re-installing more than one
product in a given category ... can significantly increase an
OEM's support costs, for the redundancy can lead to confusion among novice users." Id. p 159; see also id. p 217. That
is, a certain number of novice computer users, seeing two
browser icons, will wonder which to use when and will call the
OEM's support line. Support calls are extremely expensive
and, in the highly competitive original equipment market,
firms have a strong incentive to minimize costs. Id. p 210.

     Microsoft denies the "consumer confusion" story; it ob-
serves that some OEMs do install multiple browsers and that
executives from two OEMs that do so denied any knowledge
of consumers being confused by multiple icons. See 11/5/98
pm Tr. at 41-42 (trial testimony of Avadis Tevanian of Apple),
reprinted in 9 J.A. at 5493-94; 11/18/99 am Tr. at 69 (trial
testimony of John Soyring of IBM), reprinted in 10 J.A. at
6222.

     Other testimony, however, supports the District Court's
finding that fear of such confusion deters many OEMs from
pre-installing multiple browsers. See, e.g., 01/13/99 pm Tr. at
614-15 (deposition of Microsoft's Gayle McClain played to the
court) (explaining that redundancy of icons may be confusing
to end users); 02/18/99 pm Tr. at 46-47 (trial testimony of

John Rose of Compaq), reprinted in 21 J.A. at 14237-38
(same); 11/17/98 am Tr. at 68 (deposition of John Kies of
Packard Bell-NEC played to the court), reprinted in 9 J.A.
at 6016 (same); 11/17/98 am Tr. at 67-72 (trial testimony of
Glenn Weadock), reprinted in 9 J.A. at 6015-20 (same). Most
telling, in presentations to OEMs, Microsoft itself represent-
ed that having only one icon in a particular category would be
"less confusing for endusers." See Government's Trial Exhibit ("GX") 319 at MS98 0109453. Accordingly, we reject
Microsoft's argument that we should vacate the District
Court's Finding of Fact 159 as it relates to consumer confusion.

       As noted above, the OEM channel is one of the two
primary channels for distribution of browsers. By preventing
OEMs from removing visible means of user access to IE, the
license restriction prevents many OEMs from pre-installing a
rival browser and, therefore, protects Microsoft's monopoly
from the competition that middleware might otherwise present. Therefore, we conclude that the license restriction at
issue is anticompetitive. We defer for the moment the question whether that anticompetitive effect is outweighed by
Microsoft's proffered justifications.

       The second license provision at issue prohibits OEMs from
modifying the initial boot sequence--the process that occurs
the first time a consumer turns on the computer. Prior to
the imposition of that restriction, "among the programs that
many OEMs inserted into the boot sequence were Internet
sign-up procedures that encouraged users to choose from a
list of IAPs assembled by the OEM." Findings of Fact
p 210. Microsoft's prohibition on any alteration of the boot
sequence thus prevents OEMs from using that process to
promote the services of IAPs, many of which--at least at the
time Microsoft imposed the restriction--used Navigator rather than IE in their internet access software. See id. p 212;
GX 295, reprinted in 12 J.A. at 14533 (Upon learning of OEM
practices including boot sequence modification, Microsoft's
Chairman, Bill Gates, wrote: "Apparently a lot of OEMs are
bundling non-Microsoft browsers and coming up with offerings together with [IAPs] that get displayed on their ma-

chines in a FAR more prominent way than MSN or our
Internet browser."). Microsoft does not deny that the prohibition on modifying the boot sequence has the effect of
decreasing competition against IE by preventing OEMs from
promoting rivals' browsers. Because this prohibition has a
substantial effect in protecting Microsoft's market power, and
does so through a means other than competition on the
merits, it is anticompetitive. Again the question whether the
provision is nonetheless justified awaits later treatment.

Finally, Microsoft imposes several additional provisions
that, like the prohibition on removal of icons, prevent OEMs
from making various alterations to the desktop: Microsoft
prohibits OEMs from causing any user interface other than
the Windows desktop to launch automatically, from adding
icons or folders different in size or shape from those supplied
by Microsoft, and from using the "Active Desktop" feature to
promote third-party brands. These restrictions impose significant costs upon the OEMs; prior to Microsoft's prohibiting the practice, many OEMs would change the appearance of
the desktop in ways they found beneficial. See, e.g., Findings
of Fact p 214; GX 309, reprinted in 22 J.A. at 14551 (March
1997 letter from Hewlett-Packard to Microsoft: "We are
responsible for the cost of technical support of our customers,
including the 33% of calls we get related to the lack of quality
or confusion generated by your product.... We must have
more ability to decide how our system is presented to our end
users. If we had a choice of another supplier, based on your
actions in this area, I assure you [that you] would not be our
supplier of choice.").

The dissatisfaction of the OEM customers does not, of
course, mean the restrictions are anticompetitive. The anticompetitive effect of the license restrictions is, as Microsoft
itself recognizes, that OEMs are not able to promote rival
browsers, which keeps developers focused upon the APIs in
Windows. Findings of Fact p 212 (quoting Microsoft's Gates
as writing, "[w]inning Internet browser share is a very very
important goal for us," and emphasizing the need to prevent
OEMs from promoting both rival browsers and IAPs that
might use rivals' browsers); see also 01/13/99 Tr. at 305-06

(excerpts from deposition of James Von Holle of Gateway)
(prior to restriction Gateway had pre-installed non-IE internet registration icon that was larger than other desktop
icons). This kind of promotion is not a zero-sum game; but
for the restrictions in their licenses to use Windows, OEMs
could promote multiple IAPs and browsers. By preventing
the OEMs from doing so, this type of license restriction, like
the first two restrictions, is anticompetitive: Microsoft reduced rival browsers' usage share not by improving its own
product but, rather, by preventing OEMs from taking actions
that could increase rivals' share of usage.

  b. Microsoft's justifications for the license restrictions

 Microsoft argues that the license restrictions are legally
justified because, in imposing them, Microsoft is simply "exercising its rights as the holder of valid copyrights." Appellant's Opening Br. at 102. Microsoft also argues that the
licenses "do not unduly restrict the opportunities of Netscape
to distribute Navigator in any event." Id.

 Microsoft's primary copyright argument borders upon the
frivolous. The company claims an absolute and unfettered
right to use its intellectual property as it wishes: "[I]f
intellectual property rights have been lawfully acquired," it
says, then "their subsequent exercise cannot give rise to
antitrust liability." Appellant's Opening Br. at 105. That is
no more correct than the proposition that use of one's personal property, such as a baseball bat, cannot give rise to tort
liability. As the Federal Circuit succinctly stated: "Intellectual property rights do not confer a privilege to violate the
antitrust laws." In re Indep. Serv. Orgs. Antitrust Litig., 203
F.3d 1322, 1325 (Fed. Cir. 2000).

 Although Microsoft never overtly retreats from its bold and
incorrect position on the law, it also makes two arguments to
the effect that it is not exercising its copyright in an unreasonable manner, despite the anticompetitive consequences of
the license restrictions discussed above. In the first variation
upon its unqualified copyright defense, Microsoft cites two
cases indicating that a copyright holder may limit a licensee's

ability to engage in significant and deleterious alterations of a copyrighted work. See Gilliam v. ABC, 538 F.2d 14, 21 (2d Cir. 1976); WGN Cont'l Broad. Co. v. United Video, Inc., 693 F.2d 622, 625 (7th Cir. 1982). The relevance of those two cases for the present one is limited, however, both because those cases involved substantial alterations of a copyrighted work, see Gilliam, 538 F.2d at 18, and because in neither case was there any claim that the copyright holder was, in asserting its rights, violating the antitrust laws, see WGN Cont'l Broad., 693 F.2d at 626; see also Cmty. for Creative Non-Violence v. Reid, 846 F.2d 1485, 1498 (D.C. Cir. 1988) (noting, again in a context free of any antitrust concern, that "an author [ ] may have rights against" a licensee that "excessively mutilated or altered" the copyrighted work).

The only license restriction Microsoft seriously defends as necessary to prevent a "substantial alteration" of its copyrighted work is the prohibition on OEMs automatically launching a substitute user interface upon completion of the boot process. See Findings of Fact p 211 ("[A] few large OEMs developed programs that ran automatically at the conclusion of a new PC system's first boot sequence. These programs replaced the Windows desktop either with a user interface designed by the OEM or with Navigator's user interface."). We agree that a shell that automatically prevents the Windows desktop from ever being seen by the user is a drastic alteration of Microsoft's copyrighted work, and outweighs the marginal anticompetitive effect of prohibiting the OEMs from substituting a different interface automatically upon completion of the initial boot process. We therefore hold that this particular restriction is not an exclusionary practice that violates s 2 of the Sherman Act.

In a second variation upon its copyright defense, Microsoft argues that the license restrictions merely prevent OEMs from taking actions that would reduce substantially the value of Microsoft's copyrighted work: that is, Microsoft claims each license restriction in question is necessary to prevent OEMs from so altering Windows as to undermine "the principal value of Windows as a stable and consistent platform that supports a broad range of applications and that is familiar to users." Appellant's Opening Br. at 102. Microsoft, however, never substantiates this claim, and, because an OEM's altering the appearance of the desktop or promoting programs in the boot sequence does not affect the code already in the product, the practice does not self-evidently affect either the "stability" or the "consistency" of the platform. See Conclusions of Law, at 41; Findings of Fact p 227. Microsoft cites only one item of evidence in support of its claim that the OEMs' alterations were decreasing the value of Windows. Defendant's Trial Exhibit ("DX") 2395 at MSV0009378A, reprinted in 19 J.A. at 12575. That document, prepared by Microsoft itself, states: "there are quality issues created by OEMs who are too liberal with the pre-install process," referring to the OEMs' installation of Windows and additional software on their PCs, which the document says may result in "user concerns and confusion." To the extent the OEMs' modifications cause consumer confusion, of course, the OEMs bear the additional support costs. See Findings of Fact p 159. Therefore, we conclude Microsoft has not shown that the OEMs' liberality reduces the value of Windows except in the sense that their promotion of rival browsers undermines Microsoft's monopoly--and that is not a permissible justification for the license restrictions.

Apart from copyright, Microsoft raises one other defense of the OEM license agreements: It argues that, despite the restrictions in the OEM license, Netscape is not completely blocked from distributing its product. That claim is insufficient to shield Microsoft from liability for those restrictions because, although Microsoft did not bar its rivals from all means of distribution, it did bar them from the cost-efficient ones.

In sum, we hold that with the exception of the one restriction prohibiting automatically launched alternative interfaces, all the OEM license restrictions at issue represent uses of Microsoft's market power to protect its monopoly, unredeemed by any legitimate justification. The restrictions therefore violate s 2 of the Sherman Act.

2. Integration of IE and Windows

Although Microsoft's license restrictions have a significant effect in closing rival browsers out of one of the two primary channels of distribution, the District Court found that "Microsoft's executives believed ... its contractual restrictions placed on OEMs would not be sufficient in themselves to reverse the direction of Navigator's usage share. Consequently, in late 1995 or early 1996, Microsoft set out to bind [IE] more tightly to Windows 95 as a technical matter." Findings of Fact p 160.

Technologically binding IE to Windows, the District Court found, both prevented OEMs from pre-installing other browsers and deterred consumers from using them. In particular, having the IE software code as an irremovable part of Windows meant that pre-installing a second browser would "increase an OEM's product testing costs," because an OEM must test and train its support staff to answer calls related to every software product preinstalled on the machine; moreover, pre-installing a browser in addition to IE would to many OEMs be "a questionable use of the scarce and valuable space on a PC's hard drive." Id. p 159.

Although the District Court, in its Conclusions of Law, broadly condemned Microsoft's decision to bind "Internet Explorer to Windows with ... technological shackles," Conclusions of Law, at 39, its findings of fact in support of that conclusion center upon three specific actions Microsoft took to weld IE to Windows: excluding IE from the "Add/Remove Programs" utility; designing Windows so as in certain circumstances to override the user's choice of a default browser other than IE; and commingling code related to browsing and other code in the same files, so that any attempt to delete the files containing IE would, at the same time, cripple the operating system. As with the license restrictions, we consider first whether the suspect actions had an anticompetitive effect, and then whether Microsoft has provided a procompetitive justification for them.

a. Anticompetitive effect of integration

As a general rule, courts are properly very skeptical about claims that competition has been harmed by a dominant

firm's product design changes. See, e.g., Foremost Pro Color, Inc. v. Eastman Kodak Co., 703 F.2d 534, 544-45 (9th Cir. 1983). In a competitive market, firms routinely innovate in the hope of appealing to consumers, sometimes in the process making their products incompatible with those of rivals; the imposition of liability when a monopolist does the same thing will inevitably deter a certain amount of innovation. This is all the more true in a market, such as this one, in which the product itself is rapidly changing. See Findings of Fact p 59. Judicial deference to product innovation, however, does not mean that a monopolist's product design decisions are per se lawful. See Foremost Pro Color, 703 F.2d at 545; see also Cal. Computer Prods., 613 F.2d at 739, 744; In re IBM Peripheral EDP Devices Antitrust Litig., 481 F. Supp. 965, 1007-08 (N.D. Cal. 1979).

The District Court first condemned as anticompetitive Microsoft's decision to exclude IE from the "Add/Remove Programs" utility in Windows 98. Findings of Fact p 170. Microsoft had included IE in the Add/Remove Programs utility in Windows 95, see id. p p 175-76, but when it modified Windows 95 to produce Windows 98, it took IE out of the Add/Remove Programs utility. This change reduces the usage share of rival browsers not by making Microsoft's own browser more attractive to consumers but, rather, by discouraging OEMs from distributing rival products. See id. p 159. Because Microsoft's conduct, through something other than competition on the merits, has the effect of significantly reducing usage of rivals' products and hence protecting its own operating system monopoly, it is anticompetitive; we defer for the moment the question whether it is nonetheless justified.

Second, the District Court found that Microsoft designed Windows 98 "so that using Navigator on Windows 98 would have unpleasant consequences for users" by, in some circumstances, overriding the user's choice of a browser other than IE as his or her default browser. Id. p p 171-72. Plaintiffs argue that this override harms the competitive process by deterring consumers from using a browser other than IE even though they might prefer to do so, thereby reducing rival browsers' usage share and, hence, the ability of rival

browsers to draw developer attention away from the APIs
exposed by Windows. Microsoft does not deny, of course,
that overriding the user's preference prevents some people
from using other browsers. Because the override reduces
rivals' usage share and protects Microsoft's monopoly, it too
is anticompetitive.

Finally, the District Court condemned Microsoft's decision
to bind IE to Windows 98 "by placing code specific to Web
browsing in the same files as code that provided operating
system functions." Id. p 161; see also id. p p 174, 192. Put-
ting code supplying browsing functionality into a file with
code supplying operating system functionality "ensure[s] that
the deletion of any file containing browsing-specific routines
would also delete vital operating system routines and thus
cripple Windows...." Id. p 164. As noted above, preventing
an OEM from removing IE deters it from installing a second
browser because doing so increases the OEM's product testing and support costs; by contrast, had OEMs been able to
remove IE, they might have chosen to pre-install Navigator
alone. See id. p 159.

Microsoft denies, as a factual matter, that it commingled
browsing and non-browsing code, and it maintains the District Court's findings to the contrary are clearly erroneous.
According to Microsoft, its expert "testified without contradiction that '[t]he very same code in Windows 98 that provides Web browsing functionality' also performs essential
operating system functions--not code in the same files, but
the very same software code." Appellant's Opening Br. at 79
(citing 5 J.A. 3291-92).

Microsoft's expert did not testify to that effect "without
contradiction," however. A Government expert, Glenn Weadock, testified that Microsoft "design[ed] [IE] so that some of
the code that it uses co-resides in the same library files as
other code needed for Windows." Direct Testimony p 30.
Another Government expert likewise testified that one library
file, SHDOCVW.DLL, "is really a bundle of separate functions. It contains some functions that have to do specifically
with Web browsing, and it contains some general user inter-

face functions as well." 12/14/98 am Tr. at 60-61 (trial
testimony of Edward Felten), reprinted in 11 J.A. at 6953-54.
One of Microsoft's own documents suggests as much. See
Plaintiffs' Proposed Findings of Fact p 131.2.vii (citing GX
1686 (under seal) (Microsoft document indicating some functions in SHDOCVW.DLL can be described as "IE only,"
others can be described as "shell only" and still others can be
described as providing both "IE" and "shell" functions)).

     In view of the contradictory testimony in the record, some
of which supports the District Court's finding that Microsoft
commingled browsing and non-browsing code, we cannot conclude that the finding was clearly erroneous. See Anderson
v. City of Bessemer City, 470 U.S. 564, 573-74 (1985) ("If the
district court's account of the evidence is plausible in light of
the record viewed in its entirety, the court of appeals may not
reverse it even though convinced that had it been sitting as
the trier of fact, it would have weighed the evidence differently."). Accordingly, we reject Microsoft's argument that we
should vacate Finding of Fact 159 as it relates to the commingling of code, and we conclude that such commingling has
an anticompetitive effect; as noted above, the commingling
deters OEMs from pre-installing rival browsers, thereby reducing the rivals' usage share and, hence, developers' interest
in rivals' APIs as an alternative to the API set exposed by
Microsoft's operating system.

          b. Microsoft's justifications for integration

     Microsoft proffers no justification for two of the three
challenged actions that it took in integrating IE into Win-
dows--excluding IE from the Add/Remove Programs utility
and commingling browser and operating system code. Although Microsoft does make some general claims regarding
the benefits of integrating the browser and the operating
system, see, e.g., Direct Testimony of James Allchin p 94,
reprinted in 5 J.A. at 3321 ("Our vision of deeper levels of
technical integration is highly efficient and provides substantial benefits to customers and developers."), it neither speci-
fies nor substantiates those claims. Nor does it argue that
either excluding IE from the Add/Remove Programs utility or
commingling code achieves any integrative benefit. Plaintiffs
plainly made out a prima facie case of harm to competition in
the operating system market by demonstrating that Microsoft's actions increased its browser usage share and thus

protected its operating system monopoly from a middleware
threat and, for its part, Microsoft failed to meet its burden of
showing that its conduct serves a purpose other than protecting its operating system monopoly. Accordingly, we hold
that Microsoft's exclusion of IE from the Add/Remove Programs utility and its commingling of browser and operating
system code constitute exclusionary conduct, in violation of
s 2.

     As for the other challenged act that Microsoft took in
integrating IE into Windows--causing Windows to override
the user's choice of a default browser in certain circum-
stances--Microsoft argues that it has "valid technical reasons." Specifically, Microsoft claims that it was necessary to
design Windows to override the user's preferences when he

or she invokes one of "a few" out "of the nearly 30 means of accessing the Internet." Appellant's Opening Br. at 82. According to Microsoft:

> The Windows 98 Help system and Windows Update feature depend on ActiveX controls not supported by Navigator, and the now-discontinued Channel Bar utilized Microsoft's Channel Definition Format, which Navigator also did not support. Lastly, Windows 98 does not invoke Navigator if a user accesses the Internet through "My Computer" or "Windows Explorer" because doing so would defeat one of the purposes of those features-- enabling users to move seamlessly from local storage devices to the Web in the same browsing window.

Id. (internal citations omitted). The plaintiff bears the burden not only of rebutting a proffered justification but also of demonstrating that the anticompetitive effect of the challenged action outweighs it. In the District Court, plaintiffs appear to have done neither, let alone both; in any event, upon appeal, plaintiffs offer no rebuttal whatsoever. Accordingly, Microsoft may not be held liable for this aspect of its product design.

3. Agreements with Internet Access Providers

The District Court also condemned as exclusionary Microsoft's agreements with various IAPs. The IAPs include both Internet Service Providers, which offer consumers internet access, and Online Services ("OLSs") such as America Online

("AOL"), which offer proprietary content in addition to internet access and other services. Findings of Fact p 15. The District Court deemed Microsoft's agreements with the IAPs unlawful because:

> Microsoft licensed [IE] and the [IE] Access Kit [(of which, more below)] to hundreds of IAPs for no charge. [Findings of Fact] p p 250-51. Then, Microsoft extended valuable promotional treatment to the ten most important IAPs in exchange for their commitment to promote and distribute [IE] and to exile Navigator from the desktop. Id. p p 255-58, 261, 272, 288-90, 305-06. Finally, in exchange for efforts to upgrade existing subscribers to client software that came bundled with [IE] instead of Navigator, Microsoft granted rebates--and in some cases made outright payments--to those same IAPs. Id. p p 259-60, 295.

Conclusions of Law, at 41.

The District Court condemned Microsoft's actions in (1) offering IE free of charge to IAPs and (2) offering IAPs a bounty for each customer the IAP signs up for service using the IE browser. In effect, the court concluded that Microsoft is acting to preserve its monopoly by offering IE to IAPs at an attractive price. Similarly, the District Court held Microsoft liable for (3) developing the IE Access Kit ("IEAK"), a software package that allows an IAP to "create a distinctive identity for its service in as little as a few hours by customiz-

ing the [IE] title bar, icon, start and search pages," Findings
of Fact p 249, and (4) offering the IEAK to IAPs free of
charge, on the ground that those acts, too, helped Microsoft
preserve its monopoly. Conclusions of Law, at 41-42. Finally, the District Court found that (5) Microsoft agreed to
provide easy access to IAPs' services from the Windows
desktop in return for the IAPs' agreement to promote IE
exclusively and to keep shipments of internet access software
using Navigator under a specific percentage, typically 25%.
See Conclusions of Law, at 42 (citing Findings of Fact
p p 258, 262, 289). We address the first four items--Micro-
soft's inducements--and then its exclusive agreements with
IAPs.

     Although offering a customer an attractive deal is the
hallmark of competition, the Supreme Court has indicated

that in very rare circumstances a price may be unlawfully
low, or "predatory." See generally Brooke Group, 509 U.S. at
220-27. Plaintiffs argued before the District Court that
Microsoft's pricing was indeed predatory; but instead of
making the usual predatory pricing argument--that the pre-
dator would drive out its rivals by pricing below cost on a
particular product and then, sometime in the future, raise its
prices on that product above the competitive level in order to
recoup its earlier losses--plaintiffs argued that by pricing
below cost on IE (indeed, even paying people to take it),
Microsoft was able simultaneously to preserve its stream of
monopoly profits on Windows, thereby more than recouping
its investment in below-cost pricing on IE. The District
Court did not assign liability for predatory pricing, however,
and plaintiffs do not press this theory on appeal.

     The rare case of price predation aside, the antitrust laws do
not condemn even a monopolist for offering its product at an
attractive price, and we therefore have no warrant to condemn Microsoft for offering either IE or the IEAK free of
charge or even at a negative price. Likewise, as we said
above, a monopolist does not violate the Sherman Act simply
by developing an attractive product. See Grinnell, 384 U.S.
at 571 ("[G]rowth or development as a consequence of a
superior product [or] business acumen" is no violation.).
Therefore, Microsoft's development of the IEAK does not
violate the Sherman Act.

     We turn now to Microsoft's deals with IAPs concerning
desktop placement. Microsoft concluded these exclusive
agreements with all "the leading IAPs," Findings of Fact
p 244, including the major OLSs. Id. p 245; see also id.
p p 305, 306. The most significant of the OLS deals is with
AOL, which, when the deal was reached, "accounted for a
substantial portion of all existing Internet access subscriptions and ... attracted a very large percentage of new IAP
subscribers." Id. p 272. Under that agreement Microsoft
puts the AOL icon in the OLS folder on the Windows desktop
and AOL does not promote any non-Microsoft browser, nor
provide software using any non-Microsoft browser except at

the customer's request, and even then AOL will not supply more than 15% of its subscribers with a browser other than IE.   Id. p 289.

The Supreme Court most recently considered an antitrust challenge to an exclusive contract in Tampa Electric Co. v. Nashville Coal Co., 365 U.S. 320 (1961). That case, which involved a challenge to a requirements contract, was brought under s 3 of the Clayton Act and ss 1 and 2 of the Sherman Act. The Court held that an exclusive contract does not violate the Clayton Act unless its probable effect is to "fore-close competition in a substantial share of the line of com-merce affected." Id. at 327. The share of the market foreclosed is important because, for the contract to have an adverse effect upon competition, "the opportunities for other traders to enter into or remain in that market must be significantly limited." Id. at 328. Although "[n]either the Court of Appeals nor the District Court [had] considered in detail the question of the relevant market," id. at 330, the Court in Tampa Electric examined the record and, after defining the relevant market, determined that the contract affected less than one percent of that market. Id. at 333. After concluding, under the Clayton Act, that this share was "conservatively speaking, quite insubstantial," id., the Court went on summarily to reject the Sherman Act claims. Id. at 335 ("[I]f [the contract] does not fall within the broader prescription of s 3 of the Clayton Act it follows that it is not forbidden by those of the [Sherman Act].").

Following Tampa Electric, courts considering antitrust challenges to exclusive contracts have taken care to identify the share of the market foreclosed. Some courts have indi-cated that s 3 of the Clayton Act and s 1 of the Sherman Act require an equal degree of foreclosure before prohibiting exclusive contracts. See, e.g., Roland Mach. Co. v. Dresser Indus., Inc., 749 F.2d 380, 393 (7th Cir. 1984) (Posner, J.). Other courts, however, have held that a higher market share must be foreclosed in order to establish a violation of the Sherman Act as compared to the Clayton Act. See, e.g., Barr Labs. v. Abbott Labs., 978 F.2d 98, 110 (3d Cir.1992); 11 Herbert Hovenkamp, Antitrust Law p 1800c4 (1998) ("[T]he cases are divided, with a likely majority stating that the

Clayton Act requires a smaller showing of anticompetitive effects.").

Though what is "significant" may vary depending upon the antitrust provision under which an exclusive deal is challenged, it is clear that in all cases the plaintiff must both define the relevant market and prove the degree of foreclosure. This is a prudential requirement; exclusivity provisions in contracts may serve many useful purposes. See, e.g., Omega Envtl., Inc. v. Gilbarco, Inc., 127 F.3d 1157, 1162 (9th Cir. 1997) ("There are, however, well-recognized economic benefits to exclusive dealing arrangements, including the enhancement of interbrand competition."); Barry Wright Corp. v. ITT Grinnell Corp., 724 F.2d 227, 236 (1st Cir. 1983) (Breyer, J.) ("[V]irtually every contract to buy 'forecloses' or 'excludes' alternative sellers from some portion of the market, namely the portion consisting of what was bought."). Permitting an antitrust action to proceed any time a firm enters into an exclusive deal would both discourage a presumptively legitimate business practice and encourage costly antitrust actions. Because an exclusive deal affecting a small fraction of a market clearly cannot have the requisite harmful effect upon competition, the requirement of a significant degree of foreclosure serves a useful screening function. Cf. Frank H. Easterbrook, The Limits of Antitrust, 63 Tex. L. Rev. 1, 21-23 (1984) (discussing use of presumptions in antitrust law to screen out cases in which loss to consumers and economy is likely outweighed by cost of inquiry and risk of deterring procompetitive behavior).

In this case, plaintiffs challenged Microsoft's exclusive dealing arrangements with the IAPs under both ss 1 and 2 of the Sherman Act. The District Court, in analyzing the s 1 claim, stated, "unless the evidence demonstrates that Microsoft's agreements excluded Netscape altogether from access to roughly forty percent of the browser market, the Court should decline to find such agreements in violation of s 1." Conclusions of Law, at 52. The court recognized that Microsoft had substantially excluded Netscape from "the most efficient channels for Navigator to achieve browser usage share," id. at 53; see also Findings of Fact p 145 ("[N]o other

distribution channel for browsing software even approaches
the efficiency of OEM pre-installation and IAP bundling."),
and had relegated it to more costly and less effective methods
(such as mass mailing its browser on a disk or offering it for
download over the internet); but because Microsoft has not
"completely excluded Netscape" from reaching any potential
user by some means of distribution, however ineffective, the
court concluded the agreements do not violate s 1. Conclusions of Law, at 53. Plaintiffs did not cross-appeal this
holding.

Turning to s 2, the court stated: "the fact that Microsoft's
arrangements with various [IAPs and other] firms did not
foreclose enough of the relevant market to constitute a s 1
violation in no way detracts from the Court's assignment of
liability for the same arrangements under s 2.... [A]ll of
Microsoft's agreements, including the non-exclusive ones, severely restricted Netscape's access to those distribution channels leading most efficiently to the acquisition of browser
usage share." Conclusions of Law, at 53.

On appeal Microsoft argues that "courts have applied the
same standard to alleged exclusive dealing agreements under
both Section 1 and Section 2," Appellant's Opening Br. at 109,
and it argues that the District Court's holding of no liability
under s 1 necessarily precludes holding it liable under s 2.
The District Court appears to have based its holding with
respect to s 1 upon a "total exclusion test" rather than the
40% standard drawn from the caselaw. Even assuming the
holding is correct, however, we nonetheless reject Microsoft's
contention.

The basic prudential concerns relevant to ss 1 and 2 are
admittedly the same: exclusive contracts are commonplace--
particularly in the field of distribution--in our competitive,
market economy, and imposing upon a firm with market
power the risk of an antitrust suit every time it enters into
such a contract, no matter how small the effect, would create
an unacceptable and unjustified burden upon any such firm.
At the same time, however, we agree with plaintiffs that a
monopolist's use of exclusive contracts, in certain circum-

stances, may give rise to a s 2 violation even though the
contracts foreclose less than the roughly 40% or 50% share
usually required in order to establish a s 1 violation. See
generally Dennis W. Carlton, A General Analysis of Exclusionary Conduct and Refusal to Deal--Why Aspen and
Kodak Are Misguided, 68 Antitrust L.J. 659 (2001) (explaining various scenarios under which exclusive dealing, particularly by a dominant firm, may raise legitimate concerns about
harm to competition).

     In this case, plaintiffs allege that, by closing to rivals a
substantial percentage of the available opportunities for browser distribution, Microsoft managed to preserve its monopoly
in the market for operating systems. The IAPs constitute
one of the two major channels by which browsers can be
distributed. Findings of Fact p 242. Microsoft has exclusive
deals with "fourteen of the top fifteen access providers in
North America[, which] account for a large majority of all
Internet access subscriptions in this part of the world." Id.
p 308. By ensuring that the "majority" of all IAP subscribers
are offered IE either as the default browser or as the only
browser, Microsoft's deals with the IAPs clearly have a
significant effect in preserving its monopoly; they help keep
usage of Navigator below the critical level necessary for
Navigator or any other rival to pose a real threat to Microsoft's monopoly. See, e.g., id. p 143 (Microsoft sought to
"divert enough browser usage from Navigator to neutralize it
as a platform."); see also Carlton, at 670.

     Plaintiffs having demonstrated a harm to competition, the
burden falls upon Microsoft to defend its exclusive dealing
contracts with IAPs by providing a procompetitive justification for them. Significantly, Microsoft's only explanation for
its exclusive dealing is that it wants to keep developers
focused upon its APIs--which is to say, it wants to preserve
its power in the operating system market. 02/26/01 Ct.
Appeals Tr. at 45-47. That is not an unlawful end, but
neither is it a procompetitive justification for the specific
means here in question, namely exclusive dealing contracts
with IAPs. Accordingly, we affirm the District Court's deci-

sion holding that Microsoft's exclusive contracts with IAPs are exclusionary devices, in violation of s 2 of the Sherman Act.

4. Dealings with Internet Content Providers, Independent Software Vendors, and Apple Computer

The District Court held that Microsoft engages in exclusionary conduct in its dealings with ICPs, which develop websites; ISVs, which develop software; and Apple, which is both an OEM and a software developer. See Conclusions of Law, at 42-43 (deals with ICPs, ISVs, and Apple "supplemented Microsoft's efforts in the OEM and IAP channels"). The District Court condemned Microsoft's deals with ICPs and ISVs, stating: "By granting ICPs and ISVs free licenses to bundle [IE] with their offerings, and by exchanging other valuable inducements for their agreement to distribute, promote[,] and rely on [IE] rather than Navigator, Microsoft directly induced developers to focus on its own APIs rather than ones exposed by Navigator." Id. (citing Findings of Fact p p 334-35, 340).

With respect to the deals with ICPs, the District Court's findings do not support liability. After reviewing the ICP agreements, the District Court specifically stated that "there is not sufficient evidence to support a finding that Microsoft's promotional restrictions actually had a substantial, deleterious impact on Navigator's usage share." Findings of Fact p 332. Because plaintiffs failed to demonstrate that Microsoft's deals with the ICPs have a substantial effect upon competition, they have not proved the violation of the Sherman Act.

As for Microsoft's ISV agreements, however, the District Court did not enter a similar finding of no substantial effect. The District Court described Microsoft's deals with ISVs as follows:

> In dozens of "First Wave" agreements signed between the fall of 1997 and the spring of 1998, Microsoft has promised to give preferential support, in the form of early Windows 98 and Windows NT betas, other technical information, and the right to use certain Microsoft

seals of approval, to important ISVs that agree to certain
conditions. One of these conditions is that the ISVs use
Internet Explorer as the default browsing software for
any software they develop with a hypertext-based user
interface. Another condition is that the ISVs use Microsoft's "HTML Help," which is accessible only with Internet Explorer, to implement their applications' help systems.

Id. p 339. The District Court further found that the effect of
these deals is to "ensure [ ] that many of the most popular
Web-centric applications will rely on browsing technologies
found only in Windows," id. p 340, and that Microsoft's deals
with ISVs therefore "increase[ ] the likelihood that the millions of consumers using [applications designed by ISVs that
entered into agreements with Microsoft] will use Internet
Explorer rather than Navigator." Id. p 340.

     The District Court did not specifically identify what share
of the market for browser distribution the exclusive deals
with the ISVs foreclose. Although the ISVs are a relatively
small channel for browser distribution, they take on greater
significance because, as discussed above, Microsoft had largely foreclosed the two primary channels to its rivals. In that
light, one can tell from the record that by affecting the
applications used by "millions" of consumers, Microsoft's exclusive deals with the ISVs had a substantial effect in further
foreclosing rival browsers from the market. (Data introduced by Microsoft, see Direct Testimony of Cameron Myhr-
vold p 84, reprinted in 6 J.A. at 3922-23, and subsequently
relied upon by the District Court in its findings, see, e.g.,
Findings of Fact p 270, indicate that over the two-year period
1997-98, when Microsoft entered into the First Wave agreements, there were 40 million new users of the internet.)
Because, by keeping rival browsers from gaining widespread
distribution (and potentially attracting the attention of developers away from the APIs in Windows), the deals have a
substantial effect in preserving Microsoft's monopoly, we hold
that plaintiffs have made a prima facie showing that the deals
have an anticompetitive effect.

Of course, that Microsoft's exclusive deals have the anti-competitive effect of preserving Microsoft's monopoly does not, in itself, make them unlawful. A monopolist, like a competitive firm, may have a perfectly legitimate reason for wanting an exclusive arrangement with its distributors. Accordingly, Microsoft had an opportunity to, but did not, present the District Court with evidence demonstrating that the exclusivity provisions have some such procompetitive justification. See Conclusions of Law, at 43 (citing Findings of Fact p p 339-40) ("With respect to the ISV agreements, Microsoft has put forward no procompetitive business ends whatsoever to justify their exclusionary terms."). On appeal Microsoft likewise does not claim that the exclusivity required by the deals serves any legitimate purpose; instead, it states only that its ISV agreements reflect an attempt "to persuade ISVs to utilize Internet-related system services in Windows rather than Navigator." Appellant's Opening Br. at 114. As we explained before, however, keeping developers focused upon Windows--that is, preserving the Windows monopoly-- is a competitively neutral goal. Microsoft having offered no procompetitive justification for its exclusive dealing arrangements with the ISVs, we hold that those arrangements violate s 2 of the Sherman Act.

Finally, the District Court held that Microsoft's dealings with Apple violated the Sherman Act. See Conclusions of Law, at 42-43. Apple is vertically integrated: it makes both software (including an operating system, Mac OS), and hardware (the Macintosh line of computers). Microsoft primarily makes software, including, in addition to its operating system, a number of popular applications. One, called "Office," is a suite of business productivity applications that Microsoft has ported to Mac OS. The District Court found that "ninety percent of Mac OS users running a suite of office productivity applications [use] Microsoft's Mac Office." Findings of Fact p 344. Further, the District Court found that:

   In 1997, Apple's business was in steep decline, and many
   doubted that the company would survive much long-

er.... [M]any ISVs questioned the wisdom of continuing to spend time and money developing applications for
the Mac OS. Had Microsoft announced in the midst of
this atmosphere that it was ceasing to develop new
versions of Mac Office, a great number of ISVs, customers, developers, and investors would have interpreted the
announcement as Apple's death notice.

Id. p 344. Microsoft recognized the importance to Apple of
its continued support of Mac Office. See id. p 347 (quoting
internal Microsoft e-mail) ("[We] need a way to push these
guys[, i.e., Apple] and [threatening to cancel Mac Office] is
the only one that seems to make them move."); see also id.
("[Microsoft Chairman Bill] Gates asked whether Microsoft
could conceal from Apple in the coming month the fact that
Microsoft was almost finished developing Mac Office 97.");
id. at p 354 ("I think ... Apple should be using [IE] every-
where and if they don't do it, then we can use Office as a
club.").

    In June 1997 Microsoft Chairman Bill Gates determined
that the company's negotiations with Apple " 'have not been
going well at all.... Apple let us down on the browser by
making Netscape the standard install.' Gates then reported
that he had already called Apple's CEO ... to ask 'how we
should announce the cancellation of Mac Office....' " Id. at
p 349. The District Court further found that, within a month
of Gates' call, Apple and Microsoft had reached an agreement
pursuant to which

    Microsoft's primary obligation is to continue releasing
    up-to-date versions of Mac Office for at least five
    years.... [and] Apple has agreed ... to "bundle the
    most current version of [IE] ... with [Mac OS]"... [and
    to] "make [IE] the default [browser]".... Navigator is
    not installed on the computer hard drive during the
    default installation, which is the type of installation most
    users elect to employ.... [The] Agreement further
    provides that ... Apple may not position icons for non-
    Microsoft browsing software on the desktop of new Ma-
    cintosh PC systems or Mac OS upgrades.

Id. p p 350-52. The agreement also prohibits Apple from
encouraging users to substitute another browser for IE, and
states that Apple will "encourage its employees to use [IE]."
Id. p 352.

This exclusive deal between Microsoft and Apple has a
substantial effect upon the distribution of rival browsers. If a
browser developer ports its product to a second operating
system, such as the Mac OS, it can continue to display a
common set of APIs. Thus, usage share, not the underlying
operating system, is the primary determinant of the platform
challenge a browser may pose. Pre-installation of a browser
(which can be accomplished either by including the browser
with the operating system or by the OEM installing the
browser) is one of the two most important methods of browser distribution, and Apple had a not insignificant share of
worldwide sales of operating systems. See id. p 35 (Microsoft
has 95% of the market not counting Apple and "well above"
80% with Apple included in the relevant market). Because
Microsoft's exclusive contract with Apple has a substantial
effect in restricting distribution of rival browsers, and because (as we have described several times above) reducing
usage share of rival browsers serves to protect Microsoft's
monopoly, its deal with Apple must be regarded as anticompetitive. See Conclusions of Law, at 42 (citing Findings of
Fact p 356) ("By extracting from Apple terms that significantly diminished the usage of Navigator on the Mac OS, Microsoft helped to ensure that developers would not view Navigator as truly cross-platform middleware.").

Microsoft offers no procompetitive justification for the exclusive dealing arrangement. It makes only the irrelevant
claim that the IE-for-Mac Office deal is part of a multifaceted
set of agreements between itself and Apple, see Appellant's
Opening Br. at 61 ("Apple's 'browsing software' obligation
was [not] the quid pro quo for Microsoft's Mac Office obligation[;] ... all of the various obligations ... were part of
one 'overall agreement' between the two companies."); that
does not mean it has any procompetitive justification. Accordingly, we hold that the exclusive deal with Apple is
exclusionary, in violation of s 2 of the Sherman Act.

5. Java

     Java, a set of technologies developed by Sun Microsystems,
is another type of middleware posing a potential threat to
Windows' position as the ubiquitous platform for software
development. Findings of Fact p 28. The Java technologies
include: (1) a programming language; (2) a set of programs
written in that language, called the "Java class libraries,"
which expose APIs; (3) a compiler, which translates code
written by a developer into "bytecode"; and (4) a Java Virtual
Machine ("JVM"), which translates bytecode into instructions
to the operating system. Id. p 73. Programs calling upon the
Java APIs will run on any machine with a "Java runtime
environment," that is, Java class libraries and a JVM. Id.
p p 73, 74.

     In May 1995 Netscape agreed with Sun to distribute a copy
of the Java runtime environment with every copy of Navigator, and "Navigator quickly became the principal vehicle by
which Sun placed copies of its Java runtime environment on
the PC systems of Windows users." Id. p 76. Microsoft, too,
agreed to promote the Java technologies--or so it seemed.
For at the same time, Microsoft took steps "to maximize the
difficulty with which applications written in Java could be
ported from Windows to other platforms, and vice versa."
Conclusions of Law, at 43. Specifically, the District Court
found that Microsoft took four steps to exclude Java from
developing as a viable cross-platform threat: (a) designing a
JVM incompatible with the one developed by Sun; (b) entering into contracts, the so-called "First Wave Agreements,"
requiring major ISVs to promote Microsoft's JVM exclusively; (c) deceiving Java developers about the Windows-specific
nature of the tools it distributed to them; and (d) coercing
Intel to stop aiding Sun in improving the Java technologies.

     a. The incompatible JVM

     The District Court held that Microsoft engaged in exclu-
sionary conduct by developing and promoting its own JVM.
Conclusions of Law, at 43-44. Sun had already developed a
JVM for the Windows operating system when Microsoft
began work on its version. The JVM developed by Microsoft

allows Java applications to run faster on Windows than does
Sun's JVM, Findings of Fact p 389, but a Java application
designed to work with Microsoft's JVM does not work with
Sun's JVM and vice versa. Id. p 390. The District Court
found that Microsoft "made a large investment of engineering
resources to develop a high-performance Windows JVM," id.
p 396, and, "[b]y bundling its ... JVM with every copy of
[IE] ... Microsoft endowed its Java runtime environment
with the unique attribute of guaranteed, enduring ubiquity
across the enormous Windows installed base," id. p 397. As
explained above, however, a monopolist does not violate the
antitrust laws simply by developing a product that is incompatible with those of its rivals. See supra Section II.B.1. In
order to violate the antitrust laws, the incompatible product
must have an anticompetitive effect that outweighs any procompetitive justification for the design. Microsoft's JVM is
not only incompatible with Sun's, it allows Java applications
to run faster on Windows than does Sun's JVM. Microsoft's
faster JVM lured Java developers into using Microsoft's
developer tools, and Microsoft offered those tools deceptively,
as we discuss below. The JVM, however, does allow applications to run more swiftly and does not itself have any
anticompetitive effect. Therefore, we reverse the District
Court's imposition of liability for Microsoft's development and
promotion of its JVM.

b. The First Wave Agreements

The District Court also found that Microsoft entered into
First Wave Agreements with dozens of ISVs to use Microsoft's JVM. See Findings of Fact p 401 ("[I]n exchange for
costly technical support and other blandishments, Microsoft
induced dozens of important ISVs to make their Java applications reliant on Windows-specific technologies and to refrain
from distributing to Windows users JVMs that complied with
Sun's standards."). Again, we reject the District Court's
condemnation of low but non-predatory pricing by Microsoft.

To the extent Microsoft's First Wave Agreements with the
ISVs conditioned receipt of Windows technical information
upon the ISVs' agreement to promote Microsoft's JVM exclu-

sively, they raise a different competitive concern. The District Court found that, although not literally exclusive, the deals were exclusive in practice because they required developers to make Microsoft's JVM the default in the software they developed. Id. p 401.

While the District Court did not enter precise findings as to the effect of the First Wave Agreements upon the overall distribution of rival JVMs, the record indicates that Microsoft's deals with the major ISVs had a significant effect upon JVM promotion. As discussed above, the products of First Wave ISVs reached millions of consumers. Id. p 340. The First Wave ISVs included such prominent developers as Rational Software, see GX 970, reprinted in 15 J.A. at 9994-10000, "a world leader" in software development tools, see Direct Testimony of Michael Devlin p 2, reprinted in 5 J.A. at 3520, and Symantec, see GX 2071, reprinted in 22 J.A. at 14960-66 (sealed), which, according to Microsoft itself, is "the leading supplier of utilities such as anti-virus software," Defendant's Proposed Findings of Fact p 276, reprinted in 3 J.A. at 1689. Moreover, Microsoft's exclusive deals with the leading ISVs took place against a backdrop of foreclosure: the District Court found that "[w]hen Netscape announced in May 1995 [prior to Microsoft's execution of the First Wave Agreements] that it would include with every copy of Navigator a copy of a Windows JVM that complied with Sun's standards, it appeared that Sun's Java implementation would achieve the necessary ubiquity on Windows." Findings of Fact p 394. As discussed above, however, Microsoft undertook a number of anticompetitive actions that seriously reduced the distribution of Navigator, and the District Court found that those actions thereby seriously impeded distribution of Sun's JVM. Conclusions of Law, at 43-44. Because Microsoft's agreements foreclosed a substantial portion of the field for JVM distribution and because, in so doing, they protected Microsoft's monopoly from a middleware threat, they are anticompetitive.

Microsoft offered no procompetitive justification for the default clause that made the First Wave Agreements exclusive as a practical matter. See Findings of Fact p 401.

Because the cumulative effect of the deals is anticompetitive and because Microsoft has no procompetitive justification for them, we hold that the provisions in the First Wave Agreements requiring use of Microsoft's JVM as the default are exclusionary, in violation of the Sherman Act.

c. Deception of Java developers

Microsoft's "Java implementation" included, in addition to a JVM, a set of software development tools it created to assist ISVs in designing Java applications. The District Court found that, not only were these tools incompatible with Sun's cross-platform aspirations for Java--no violation, to be sure--but Microsoft deceived Java developers regarding the Windows-specific nature of the tools. Microsoft's tools included "certain 'keywords' and 'compiler directives' that could only be executed properly by Microsoft's version of the Java runtime environment for Windows." Id. p 394; see also Direct Testimony of James Gosling p 58, reprinted in 21 J.A. at 13959 (Microsoft added "programming instructions ... that alter the behavior of the code."). As a result, even Java "developers who were opting for portability over performance ... unwittingly [wrote] Java applications that [ran] only on Windows." Conclusions of Law, at 43. That is, developers who relied upon Microsoft's public commitment to cooperate with Sun and who used Microsoft's tools to develop what Microsoft led them to believe were cross-platform applications ended up producing applications that would run only on the Windows operating system.

When specifically accused by a PC Week reporter of fragmenting Java standards so as to prevent cross-platform uses, Microsoft denied the accusation and indicated it was only "adding rich platform support" to what remained a cross-platform implementation. An e-mail message internal to Microsoft, written shortly after the conversation with the reporter, shows otherwise:

> [O]k, i just did a followup call.... [The reporter] liked that i kept pointing customers to w3c standards [(commonly observed internet protocols)].... [but] he accused us of being schizo with this vs. our java approach, i said

he misunderstood [--] that [with Java] we are merely
trying to add rich platform support to an interop lay-
er.... this plays well.... at this point its [sic] not good
to create MORE noise around our win32 java classes.
instead we should just quietly grow j [(Microsoft's
development tools)] share and assume that people will
take more advantage of our classes without ever realizing
they are building win32-only java apps.

GX 1332, reprinted in 22 J.A. at 14922-23.

Finally, other Microsoft documents confirm that Microsoft
intended to deceive Java developers, and predicted that the
effect of its actions would be to generate Windows-dependent
Java applications that their developers believed would be
cross-platform; these documents also indicate that Microsoft's ultimate objective was to thwart Java's threat to Microsoft's monopoly in the market for operating systems. One
Microsoft document, for example, states as a strategic goal:
"Kill cross-platform Java by grow[ing] the polluted Java
market." GX 259, reprinted in 22 J.A. at 14514; see also id.
("Cross-platform capability is by far the number one reason
for choosing/using Java.") (emphasis in original).

Microsoft's conduct related to its Java developer tools
served to protect its monopoly of the operating system in a
manner not attributable either to the superiority of the
operating system or to the acumen of its makers, and therefore was anticompetitive. Unsurprisingly, Microsoft offers no
procompetitive explanation for its campaign to deceive developers. Accordingly, we conclude this conduct is exclusionary,
in violation of s 2 of the Sherman Act.

d. The threat to Intel

The District Court held that Microsoft also acted unlawfully with respect to Java by using its "monopoly power to
prevent firms such as Intel from aiding in the creation of
cross-platform interfaces." Conclusions of Law, at 43. In
1995 Intel was in the process of developing a high-
performance, Windows-compatible JVM. Microsoft wanted
Intel to abandon that effort because a fast, cross-platform

JVM would threaten Microsoft's monopoly in the operating
system market. At an August 1995 meeting, Microsoft's
Gates told Intel that its "cooperation with Sun and Netscape
to develop a Java runtime environment ... was one of the
issues threatening to undermine cooperation between Intel
and Microsoft." Findings of Fact p 396. Three months
later, "Microsoft's Paul Maritz told a senior Intel executive
that Intel's [adaptation of its multimedia software to comply
with] Sun's Java standards was as inimical to Microsoft as
Microsoft's support for non-Intel microprocessors would be to
Intel." Id. p 405.

Intel nonetheless continued to undertake initiatives related
to Java. By 1996 "Intel had developed a JVM designed to
run well ... while complying with Sun's cross-platform standards." Id. p 396. In April of that year, Microsoft again
urged Intel not to help Sun by distributing Intel's fast, Sun-
compliant JVM. Id. And Microsoft threatened Intel that if
it did not stop aiding Sun on the multimedia front, then
Microsoft would refuse to distribute Intel technologies bundled with Windows. Id. p 404.

Intel finally capitulated in 1997, after Microsoft delivered
the coup de grace.

> [O]ne of Intel's competitors, called AMD, solicited sup-
> port from Microsoft for its "3DX" technology.... Mi-
> crosoft's Allchin asked Gates whether Microsoft should
> support 3DX, despite the fact that Intel would oppose it.
> Gates responded: "If Intel has a real problem with us
> supporting this then they will have to stop supporting
> Java Multimedia the way they are. I would gladly give
> up supporting this if they would back off from their work
> on JAVA."

Id. p 406.

Microsoft's internal documents and deposition testimony
confirm both the anticompetitive effect and intent of its
actions. See, e.g., GX 235, reprinted in 22 J.A. at 14502
(Microsoft executive, Eric Engstrom, included among Microsoft's goals for Intel: "Intel to stop helping Sun create Java

Multimedia APIs, especially ones that run well ... on Windows."); Deposition of Eric Engstrom at 179 ("We were successful [in convincing Intel to stop aiding Sun] for some period of time.").

Microsoft does not deny the facts found by the District Court, nor does it offer any procompetitive justification for pressuring Intel not to support cross-platform Java. Microsoft lamely characterizes its threat to Intel as "advice." The District Court, however, found that Microsoft's "advice" to Intel to stop aiding cross-platform Java was backed by the threat of retaliation, and this conclusion is supported by the evidence cited above. Therefore we affirm the conclusion that Microsoft's threats to Intel were exclusionary, in violation of s 2 of the Sherman Act.

6. Course of Conduct

The District Court held that, apart from Microsoft's specific acts, Microsoft was liable under s 2 based upon its general "course of conduct." In reaching this conclusion the court relied upon Continental Ore Co. v. Union Carbide & Carbon Corp., 370 U.S. 690, 699 (1962), where the Supreme Court stated, "[i]n [Sherman Act cases], plaintiffs should be given the full benefit of their proof without tightly compartmentalizing the various factual components and wiping the slate clean after scrutiny of each."

Microsoft points out that Continental Ore and the other cases cited by plaintiffs in support of "course of conduct" liability all involve conspiracies among multiple firms, not the conduct of a single firm; in that setting the "course of conduct" is the conspiracy itself, for which all the participants may be held liable. See Appellant's Opening Br. at 112-13. Plaintiffs respond that, as a policy matter, a monopolist's unilateral "campaign of [acts intended to exclude a rival] that in the aggregate has the requisite impact" warrants liability even if the acts viewed individually would be lawful for want of a significant effect upon competition. Appellees' Br. at 82-83.

We need not pass upon plaintiffs' argument, however, because the District Court did not point to any series of acts, each of which harms competition only slightly but the cumula-

tive effect of which is significant enough to form an independent basis for liability. The "course of conduct" section of the District Court's opinion contains, with one exception, only broad, summarizing conclusions. See, e.g., Conclusions of Law, at 44 ("Microsoft placed an oppressive thumb on the scale of competitive fortune...."). The only specific acts to which the court refers are Microsoft's expenditures in promoting its browser, see id. ("Microsoft has expended wealth and foresworn opportunities to realize more...."), which we have explained are not in themselves unlawful. Because the District Court identifies no other specific acts as a basis for "course of conduct" liability, we reverse its conclusion that Microsoft's course of conduct separately violates s 2 of the Sherman Act.

C. Causation

As a final parry, Microsoft urges this court to reverse on the monopoly maintenance claim, because plaintiffs never established a causal link between Microsoft's anticompetitive conduct, in particular its foreclosure of Netscape's and Java's distribution channels, and the maintenance of Microsoft's operating system monopoly. See Findings of Fact p 411 ("There is insufficient evidence to find that, absent Micro-soft's actions, Navigator and Java already would have ignited genuine competition in the market for Intel-compatible PC operating systems."). This is the flip side of Microsoft's earlier argument that the District Court should have included middleware in the relevant market. According to Microsoft, the District Court cannot simultaneously find that middle-ware is not a reasonable substitute and that Microsoft's exclusionary conduct contributed to the maintenance of mo-nopoly power in the operating system market. Microsoft claims that the first finding depended on the court's view that middleware does not pose a serious threat to Windows, see supra Section II.A, while the second finding required the court to find that Navigator and Java would have developed into serious enough cross-platform threats to erode the appli-cations barrier to entry. We disagree.

Microsoft points to no case, and we can find none, standing for the proposition that, as to s 2 liability in an equitable enforcement action, plaintiffs must present direct proof that a defendant's continued monopoly power is precisely attributable to its anticompetitive conduct. As its lone authority, Microsoft cites the following passage from Professor Areeda's antitrust treatise: "The plaintiff has the burden of pleading, introducing evidence, and presumably proving by a preponderance of the evidence that reprehensible behavior has contributed significantly to the ... maintenance of the monopoly." 3 Phillip E. Areeda & Herbert Hovenkamp, Antitrust Law p 650c, at 69 (1996) (emphasis added).

But, with respect to actions seeking injunctive relief, the authors of that treatise also recognize the need for courts to infer "causation" from the fact that a defendant has engaged in anticompetitive conduct that "reasonably appear[s] capable of making a significant contribution to ... maintaining monopoly power." Id. p 651c, at 78; see also Morgan v. Ponder, 892 F.2d 1355, 1363 (8th Cir. 1989); Barry Wright, 724 F.2d at 230. To require that s 2 liability turn on a plaintiff's ability or inability to reconstruct the hypothetical marketplace absent a defendant's anticompetitive conduct would only encourage monopolists to take more and earlier anticompetitive action.

We may infer causation when exclusionary conduct is aimed at producers of nascent competitive technologies as well as when it is aimed at producers of established substitutes. Admittedly, in the former case there is added uncertainty, inasmuch as nascent threats are merely potential substitutes. But the underlying proof problem is the same--neither plaintiffs nor the court can confidently reconstruct a product's hypothetical technological development in a world absent the defendant's exclusionary conduct. To some degree, "the defendant is made to suffer the uncertain consequences of its own undesirable conduct." 3 Areeda & Hovenkamp, Antitrust Law p 651c, at 78.

Given this rather edentulous test for causation, the question in this case is not whether Java or Navigator would

actually have developed into viable platform substitutes, but
(1) whether as a general matter the exclusion of nascent
threats is the type of conduct that is reasonably capable of
contributing significantly to a defendant's continued monopoly
power and (2) whether Java and Navigator reasonably constituted nascent threats at the time Microsoft engaged in the
anticompetitive conduct at issue. As to the first, suffice it to
say that it would be inimical to the purpose of the Sherman
Act to allow monopolists free reign to squash nascent, albeit
unproven, competitors at will--particularly in industries
marked by rapid technological advance and frequent para-
digm shifts. Findings of Fact p p 59-60. As to the second,
the District Court made ample findings that both Navigator
and Java showed potential as middleware platform threats.
Findings of Fact p p 68-77. Counsel for Microsoft admitted
as much at oral argument. 02/26/01 Ct. Appeals Tr. at 27
("There are no constraints on output. Marginal costs are
essentially zero. And there are to some extent network
effects. So a company like Netscape founded in 1994 can be
by the middle of 1995 clearly a potentially lethal competitor to
Windows because it can supplant its position in the market
because of the characteristics of these markets.").

Microsoft's concerns over causation have more purchase in
connection with the appropriate remedy issue, i.e., whether
the court should impose a structural remedy or merely enjoin
the offensive conduct at issue. As we point out later in this
opinion, divestiture is a remedy that is imposed only with
great caution, in part because its long-term efficacy is rarely
certain. See infra Section V.E. Absent some measure of
confidence that there has been an actual loss to competition
that needs to be restored, wisdom counsels against adopting
radical structural relief. See 3 Areeda & Hovenkamp, Antitrust Law p 653b, at 91-92 ("[M]ore extensive equitable relief,
particularly remedies such as divestiture designed to eliminate the monopoly altogether, raise more serious questions
and require a clearer indication of a significant causal connection between the conduct and creation or maintenance of the
market power."). But these queries go to questions of remedy, not liability. In short, causation affords Microsoft no

defense to liability for its unlawful actions undertaken to maintain its monopoly in the operating system market.

III. Attempted Monopolization

Microsoft further challenges the District Court's determination of liability for "attempt[ing] to monopolize ... any part of the trade or commerce among the several States." 15 U.S.C. s 2 (1997). To establish a s 2 violation for attempted monopolization, "a plaintiff must prove (1) that the defendant has engaged in predatory or anticompetitive conduct with (2) a specific intent to monopolize and (3) a dangerous probability of achieving monopoly power." Spectrum Sports, Inc. v. McQuillan, 506 U.S. 447, 456 (1993); see also Times-Picayune Pub. Co. v. United States, 345 U.S. 594, 626 (1953); Lorain Journal Co. v. United States, 342 U.S. 143, 153-55 (1951). Because a deficiency on any one of the three will defeat plaintiffs' claim, we look no further than plaintiffs' failure to prove a dangerous probability of achieving monopoly power in the putative browser market.

The determination whether a dangerous probability of success exists is a particularly fact-intensive inquiry. Because the Sherman Act does not identify the activities that constitute the offense of attempted monopolization, the court "must examine the facts of each case, mindful that the determination of what constitutes an attempt, as Justice Holmes explained, 'is a question of proximity and degree.' " United States v. Am. Airlines, Inc., 743 F.2d 1114, 1118 (5th Cir. 1984) (quoting Swift & Co. v. United States, 196 U.S. 375, 402 (1904)). The District Court determined that "[t]he evidence supports the conclusion that Microsoft's actions did pose such a danger." Conclusions of Law, at 45. Specifically, the District Court concluded that "Netscape's assent to Microsoft's market division proposal would have, instanter, resulted in Microsoft's attainment of monopoly power in a second market," and that "the proposal itself created a dangerous probability of that result." Conclusions of Law, at 46 (citation omitted). The District Court further concluded that "the predatory course of conduct Microsoft has pursued since June

of 1995 has revived the dangerous probability that Microsoft
will attain monopoly power in a second market." Id.

     At the outset we note a pervasive flaw in the District
Court's and plaintiffs' discussion of attempted monopolization.
Simply put, plaintiffs have made the same argument under
two different headings--monopoly maintenance and attempted monopolization. They have relied upon Microsoft's s 2
liability for monopolization of the operating system market as
a presumptive indicator of attempted monopolization of an
entirely different market. The District Court implicitly ac-
cepted this approach: It agreed with plaintiffs that the events
that formed the basis for the s 2 monopolization claim "warrant[ed] additional liability as an illegal attempt to amass
monopoly power in 'the browser market.' " Id. at 45 (emphasis added). Thus, plaintiffs and the District Court failed to
recognize the need for an analysis wholly independent of the
conclusions and findings on monopoly maintenance.

     To establish a dangerous probability of success, plaintiffs
must as a threshold matter show that the browser market can
be monopolized, i.e., that a hypothetical monopolist in that
market could enjoy market power. This, in turn, requires
plaintiffs (1) to define the relevant market and (2) to demonstrate that substantial barriers to entry protect that market.
Because plaintiffs have not carried their burden on either
prong, we reverse without remand.

A.   Relevant Market

     A court's evaluation of an attempted monopolization claim
must include a definition of the relevant market. See Spectrum Sports, 506 U.S. at 455-56. Such a definition estab-
lishes a context for evaluating the defendant's actions as well
as for measuring whether the challenged conduct presented a
dangerous probability of monopolization. See id. The District Court omitted this element of the Spectrum Sports
inquiry.

     Defining a market for an attempted monopolization claim
involves the same steps as defining a market for a monopoly
maintenance claim, namely a detailed description of the purpose of a browser--what functions may be included and what

are not--and an examination of the substitutes that are part
of the market and those that are not. See also supra Section
II.A. The District Court never engaged in such an analysis
nor entered detailed findings defining what a browser is or
what products might constitute substitutes. In the Findings
of Fact, the District Court (in a section on whether IE and
Windows are separate products) stated only that "a Web
browser provides the ability for the end user to select,
retrieve, and perceive resources on the Web." Findings of
Fact p 150. Furthermore, in discussing attempted monopolization in its Conclusions of Law, the District Court failed to
demonstrate analytical rigor when it employed varying and
imprecise references to the "market for browsing technology
for Windows," "the browser market," and "platform-level
browsing software." Conclusions of Law, at 45.

     Because the determination of a relevant market is a factual
question to be resolved by the District Court, see, e.g., All
Care Nursing Serv., Inc. v. High Tech Staffing Servs., Inc.,
135 F.3d 740, 749 (11th Cir. 1998); Tunis Bros. Co., Inc. v.
Ford Motor Co., 952 F.2d 715, 722-23 (3d Cir. 1991); West-
man Comm'n Co. v. Hobart Int'l, Inc., 796 F.2d 1216, 1220
(10th Cir. 1986), we would normally remand the case so that
the District Court could formulate an appropriate definition.
See Pullman-Standard v. Swint, 456 U.S. 273, 291-92 & n.22
(1982); Janini v. Kuwait Univ., 43 F.3d 1534, 1537 (D.C. Cir.
1995); Palmer v. Shultz, 815 F.2d 84, 103 (D.C. Cir. 1987). A
remand on market definition is unnecessary, however, because the District Court's imprecision is directly traceable to
plaintiffs' failure to articulate and identify evidence before the
District Court as to (1) what constitutes a browser (i.e., what
are the technological components of or functionalities provided by a browser) and (2) why certain other products are not
reasonable substitutes (e.g., browser shells or viewers for
individual internet extensions, such as Real Audio Player or
Adobe Acrobat Reader). See Plaintiffs' Joint Proposed Findings of Fact, at 817-19, reprinted in 2 J.A. at 1480-82;
Plaintiffs' Joint Proposed Conclusions of Law s IV (No. 98-
1232); see also Lee v. Interstate Fire & Cas. Co., 86 F.3d 101,

105 (7th Cir. 1996) (stating that remand for development of a factual record is inappropriate where plaintiff failed to meet burden of persuasion and never suggested that additional evidence was necessary). Indeed, when plaintiffs in their Proposed Findings of Fact attempted to define a relevant market for the attempt claim, they pointed only to their separate products analysis for the tying claim. See, e.g., Plaintiffs' Joint Proposed Findings of Fact, at 818, reprinted in 2 J.A. at 1481. However, the separate products analysis for tying purposes is not a substitute for the type of market definition that Spectrum Sports requires. See infra Section IV.A.

Plaintiffs' proposed findings and the District Court's actual findings on attempted monopolization pale in comparison to their counterparts on the monopoly maintenance claim. Compare Findings of Fact p 150, and Plaintiffs' Joint Proposed Findings of Fact, at 817-819, reprinted in 2 J.A. at 1480-82, with Findings of Fact p p 18-66, and Plaintiffs' Joint Proposed Findings of Fact, at 20-31, reprinted in 1 J.A. at 658-69. Furthermore, in their brief and at oral argument before this court, plaintiffs did nothing to clarify or ameliorate this deficiency. See, e.g., Appellees' Br. at 93-94.`

B.   Barriers to Entry

Because a firm cannot possess monopoly power in a market unless that market is also protected by significant barriers to entry, see supra Section II.A, it follows that a firm cannot threaten to achieve monopoly power in a market unless that market is, or will be, similarly protected. See Spectrum Sports, 506 U.S. at 456 ("In order to determine whether there is a dangerous probability of monopolization, courts have found it necessary to consider ... the defendant's ability to lessen or destroy competition in that market.") (citing cases). Plaintiffs have the burden of establishing barriers to entry into a properly defined relevant market. See 2A Phillip E. Areeda et al., Antitrust Law p 420b, at 57-59 (1995); 3A Phillip E. Areeda & Herbert Hovenkamp, Antitrust Law p 807g, at 361-62 (1996); see also Neumann v. Reinforced

Earth Co., 786 F.2d 424, 429 (D.C. Cir. 1986). Plaintiffs must
not only show that barriers to entry protect the properly
defined browser market, but that those barriers are "significant." See United States v. Baker Hughes Inc., 908 F.2d 981,
987 (D.C. Cir. 1990). Whether there are significant barriers
to entry cannot, of course, be answered absent an appropriate
market definition; thus, plaintiffs' failure on that score alone
is dispositive. But even were we to assume a properly
defined market, for example browsers consisting of a graphi-
cal interface plus internet protocols, plaintiffs nonetheless
failed to carry their burden on barriers to entry.

    Contrary to plaintiffs' contention on appeal, see Appellees'
Br. at 91-93, none of the District Court's statements constitutes a finding of barriers to entry into the web browser
market. Finding of Fact 89 states:

> At the time Microsoft presented its proposal, Navigator
> was the only browser product with a significant share of
> the market and thus the only one with the potential to
> weaken the applications barrier to entry. Thus, had it
> convinced Netscape to accept its offer of a "special
> relationship," Microsoft quickly would have gained such
> control over the extensions and standards that network-
> centric applications (including Web sites) employ as to
> make it all but impossible for any future browser rival to
> lure appreciable developer interest away from Micro-
> soft's platform.

    This finding is far too speculative to establish that compet-
ing browsers would be unable to enter the market, or that
Microsoft would have the power to raise the price of its
browser above, or reduce the quality of its browser below, the
competitive level. Moreover, it is ambiguous insofar as it
appears to focus on Microsoft's response to the perceived
platform threat rather than the browser market. Finding of
Fact 144, on which plaintiffs also rely, is part of the District
Court's discussion of Microsoft's alleged anticompetitive actions to eliminate the platform threat posed by Netscape
Navigator. This finding simply describes Microsoft's reliance

on studies indicating consumers' reluctance to switch browsers, a reluctance not shown to be any more than that which
stops consumers from switching brands of cereal. Absent
more extensive and definitive factual findings, the District
Court's legal conclusions about entry barriers amount to
nothing more than speculation.

In contrast to their minimal effort on market definition,
plaintiffs did at least offer proposed findings of fact suggesting that the possibility of network effects could potentially
create barriers to entry into the browser market. See Plaintiffs' Joint Proposed Findings of Fact, at 822-23, 825-27,
reprinted in 2 J.A. at 1485-86, 1488-90. The District Court
did not adopt those proposed findings. See Findings of Fact
p 89. However, the District Court did acknowledge the possibility of a different kind of entry barrier in its Conclusions of
Law:

> In the time it would have taken an aspiring entrant to
> launch a serious effort to compete against Internet Ex-
> plorer, Microsoft could have erected the same type of
> barrier that protects its existing monopoly power by
> adding proprietary extensions to the browsing software
> under its control and by extracting commitments from
> OEMs, IAPs and others similar to the ones discussed in
> [the monopoly maintenance section].

Conclusions of Law, at 46 (emphasis added).

Giving plaintiffs and the District Court the benefit of the
doubt, we might remand if the possible existence of entry
barriers resulting from the possible creation and exploitation
of network effects in the browser market were the only
concern. That is not enough to carry the day, however,
because the District Court did not make two key findings: (1)
that network effects were a necessary or even probable,
rather than merely possible, consequence of high market
share in the browser market and (2) that a barrier to entry
resulting from network effects would be "significant" enough
to confer monopoly power. Again, these deficiencies are in
large part traceable to plaintiffs' own failings. As to the first
point, the District Court's use of the phrase "could have"

reflects the same uncertainty articulated in testimony cited in plaintiffs' proposed findings. See Plaintiffs' Joint Proposed Findings of Fact, at 822 (citing testimony of Frederick Warren-Boulton), at 826 (citing testimony of Franklin Fisher), reprinted in 2 J.A. at 1485, 1489. As to the second point, the cited testimony in plaintiffs' proposed findings offers little more than conclusory statements. See id. at 822-27, reprinted in 2 J.A. at 1485-90. The proffered testimony contains no evidence regarding the cost of "porting" websites to different browsers or the potentially different economic incentives facing ICPs, as opposed to ISVs, in their decision to incur costs to do so. Simply invoking the phrase "network effects" without pointing to more evidence does not suffice to carry plaintiffs' burden in this respect.

Any doubt that we may have had regarding remand instead of outright reversal on the barriers to entry question was dispelled by plaintiffs' arguments on attempted monopolization before this court. Not only did plaintiffs fail to articulate a website barrier to entry theory in either their brief or at oral argument, they failed to point the court to evidence in the record that would support a finding that Microsoft would likely erect significant barriers to entry upon acquisition of a dominant market share.

Plaintiffs did not devote the same resources to the attempted monopolization claim as they did to the monopoly maintenance claim. But both claims require evidentiary and theoretical rigor. Because plaintiffs failed to make their case on attempted monopolization both in the District Court and before this court, there is no reason to give them a second chance to flesh out a claim that should have been fleshed out the first time around. Accordingly, we reverse the District Court's determination of s 2 liability for attempted monopolization.

IV. Tying

Microsoft also contests the District Court's determination of liability under s 1 of the Sherman Act. The District Court concluded that Microsoft's contractual and technological bun-

dling of the IE web browser (the "tied" product) with its
Windows operating system ("OS") (the "tying" product) resulted in a tying arrangement that was per se unlawful.
Conclusions of Law, at 47-51. We hold that the rule of
reason, rather than per se analysis, should govern the legality
of tying arrangements involving platform software products.
The Supreme Court has warned that " '[i]t is only after
considerable experience with certain business relationships
that courts classify them as per se violations....' " Broad.
Music, Inc. v. CBS, 441 U.S. 1, 9 (1979) (quoting United
States v. Topco Assocs., 405 U.S. 596, 607-08 (1972)). While
every "business relationship" will in some sense have unique
features, some represent entire, novel categories of dealings.
As we shall explain, the arrangement before us is an example
of the latter, offering the first up-close look at the technological integration of added functionality into software that serves
as a platform for third-party applications. There being no
close parallel in prior antitrust cases, simplistic application of
per se tying rules carries a serious risk of harm. Accordingly, we vacate the District Court's finding of a per se tying
violation and remand the case. Plaintiffs may on remand
pursue their tying claim under the rule of reason.

The facts underlying the tying allegation substantially overlap with those set forth in Section II.B in connection with the
s 2 monopoly maintenance claim. The key District Court
findings are that (1) Microsoft required licensees of Windows
95 and 98 also to license IE as a bundle at a single price,
Findings of Fact p p 137, 155, 158; (2) Microsoft refused to
allow OEMs to uninstall or remove IE from the Windows
desktop, id. p p 158, 203, 213; (3) Microsoft designed Windows 98 in a way that withheld from consumers the ability to
remove IE by use of the Add/Remove Programs utility, id.
p 170; cf. id. p 165 (stating that IE was subject to Add/Re-
move Programs utility in Windows 95); and (4) Microsoft
designed Windows 98 to override the user's choice of default
web browser in certain circumstances, id. p p 171, 172. The
court found that these acts constituted a per se tying violation. Conclusions of Law, at 47-51. Although the District
Court also found that Microsoft commingled operating sys-

tem-only and browser-only routines in the same library files,
Findings of Fact p p 161, 164, it did not include this as a basis
for tying liability despite plaintiffs' request that it do so,
Plaintiffs' Proposed Findings of Fact, p p 131-32, reprinted in
2 J.A. at 941-47.

There are four elements to a per se tying violation: (1) the
tying and tied goods are two separate products; (2) the
defendant has market power in the tying product market; (3)
the defendant affords consumers no choice but to purchase
the tied product from it; and (4) the tying arrangement
forecloses a substantial volume of commerce. See Eastman
Kodak Co. v. Image Tech. Servs., Inc., 504 U.S. 451, 461-62
(1992); Jefferson Parish Hosp. Dist. No. 2 v. Hyde, 466 U.S.
2, 12-18 (1984).

Microsoft does not dispute that it bound Windows and IE
in the four ways the District Court cited. Instead it argues
that Windows (the tying good) and IE browsers (the tied
good) are not "separate products," Appellant's Opening Br. at
69-79, and that it did not substantially foreclose competing
browsers from the tied product market, id. at 79-83. (Microsoft also contends that it does not have monopoly power in
the tying product market, id. at 84-96, but, for reasons given
in Section II.A, we uphold the District Court's finding to the
contrary.)

We first address the separate-products inquiry, a source of
much argument between the parties and of confusion in the
cases. Our purpose is to highlight the poor fit between the
separate-products test and the facts of this case. We then
offer further reasons for carving an exception to the per se
rule when the tying product is platform software. In the
final section we discuss the District Court's inquiry if plaintiffs pursue a rule of reason claim on remand.

A.   Separate-Products Inquiry Under the Per Se Test

The requirement that a practice involve two separate products before being condemned as an illegal tie started as a
purely linguistic requirement: unless products are separate,
one cannot be "tied" to the other. Indeed, the nature of the

products involved in early tying cases--intuitively distinct
items such as a movie projector and a film, Motion Picture
Patents Co. v. Universal Film Mfg. Co., 243 U.S. 502 (1917)--
led courts either to disregard the separate-products question,
see, e.g., United Shoe Mach. Corp. v. United States, 258 U.S.
451 (1922), or to discuss it only in passing, see, e.g., Motion
Picture Patents, 243 U.S. at 508, 512, 518. It was not until
Times-Picayune Publishing Co. v. United States, 345 U.S.
594 (1953), that the separate-products issue became a distinct
element of the test for an illegal tie. Id. at 614. Even that
case engaged in a rather cursory inquiry into whether ads
sold in the morning edition of a paper were a separate
product from ads sold in the evening edition.

     The first case to give content to the separate-products test
was Jefferson Parish, 466 U.S. 2. That case addressed a
tying arrangement in which a hospital conditioned surgical
care at its facility on the purchase of anesthesiological services from an affiliated medical group. The facts were a
challenge for casual separate-products analysis because the
tied service--anesthesia--was neither intuitively distinct from
nor intuitively contained within the tying service--surgical
care. A further complication was that, soon after the Court
enunciated the per se rule for tying liability in International
Salt Co. v. United States, 332 U.S. 392, 396 (1947), and
Northern Pacific Railway Co. v. United States, 356 U.S. 1, 5-
7 (1958), new economic research began to cast doubt on the
assumption, voiced by the Court when it established the rule,
that " 'tying agreements serve hardly any purpose beyond the
suppression of competition,' " id. at 6 (quoting Standard Oil
of Cal. v. United States, 337 U.S. 293, 305-06 (1949)); see also
Jefferson Parish, 466 U.S. at 15 n.23 (citing materials); Fortner Enters. v. U.S. Steel Corp., 394 U.S. 495, 524-25 (1969)
(Fortas, J., dissenting) ("Fortner I").

     The Jefferson Parish Court resolved the matter in two
steps. First, it clarified that "the answer to the question
whether one or two products are involved" does not turn "on
the functional relation between them...." Jefferson Parish,
466 U.S. at 19; see also id. at 19 n.30. In other words, the
mere fact that two items are complements, that "one ... is

useless without the other," id., does not make them a single "product" for purposes of tying law. Accord Eastman Kodak, 504 U.S. at 463. Second, reasoning that the "definitional question [whether two distinguishable products are involved] depends on whether the arrangement may have the type of competitive consequences addressed by the rule [against tying]," Jefferson Parish, 466 U.S. at 21, the Court decreed that "no tying arrangement can exist unless there is a sufficient demand for the purchase of anesthesiological services separate from hospital services to identify a distinct product market in which it is efficient to offer anesthesiological services separately from hospital service," id. at 21-22 (emphasis added); accord Eastman Kodak, 504 U.S. at 462.

The Court proceeded to examine direct and indirect evidence of consumer demand for the tied product separate from the tying product. Direct evidence addresses the question whether, when given a choice, consumers purchase the tied good from the tying good maker, or from other firms. The Court took note, for example, of testimony that patients and surgeons often requested specific anesthesiologists not associated with a hospital. Jefferson Parish, 466 U.S. at 22. Indirect evidence includes the behavior of firms without market power in the tying good market, presumably on the notion that (competitive) supply follows demand. If competitive firms always bundle the tying and tied goods, then they are a single product. See id. at 22 n.36; see also Eastman Kodak, 504 U.S. at 462; Fortner I, 394 U.S. at 525 (Fortas, J., dissenting), cited in Jefferson Parish, 466 U.S. at 12, 22 n.35; United States v. Jerrold Elecs. Corp., 187 F. Supp. 545, 559 (E.D. Pa. 1960), aff'd per curiam, 365 U.S. 567 (1961); 10 Phillip E. Areeda et al., Antitrust Law p 1744, at 197-201 (1996). Here the Court noted that only 27% of anesthesiologists in markets other than the defendant's had financial relationships with hospitals, and that, unlike radiologists and pathologists, anesthesiologists were not usually employed by hospitals, i.e., bundled with hospital services. Jefferson Parish, 466 U.S. at 22 n.36. With both direct and indirect

evidence concurring, the Court determined that hospital sur-
gery and anesthesiological services were distinct goods.

To understand the logic behind the Court's consumer demand test, consider first the postulated harms from tying.
The core concern is that tying prevents goods from competing
directly for consumer choice on their merits, i.e., being select-
ed as a result of "buyers' independent judgment," id. at 13
(internal quotes omitted). With a tie, a buyer's "freedom to
select the best bargain in the second market [could be]
impaired by his need to purchase the tying product, and
perhaps by an inability to evaluate the true cost of either
product...." Id. at 15. Direct competition on the merits of
the tied product is foreclosed when the tying product either is
sold only in a bundle with the tied product or, though offered
separately, is sold at a bundled price, so that the buyer pays
the same price whether he takes the tied product or not. In
both cases, a consumer buying the tying product becomes
entitled to the tied product; he will therefore likely be
unwilling to buy a competitor's version of the tied product
even if, making his own price/quality assessment, that is what
he would prefer.

But not all ties are bad. Bundling obviously saves distribution and consumer transaction costs. 9 Phillip E. Areeda,
Antitrust Law p 1703g2, at 51-52 (1991). This is likely to be
true, to take some examples from the computer industry, with
the integration of math co-processors and memory into microprocessor chips and the inclusion of spell checkers in word
processors. 11/10/98 pm Tr. at 18-19 (trial testimony of
Steven McGeady of Intel), reprinted in 9 J.A. at 5581-82
(math co-processor); Cal. Computer Prods., Inc. v. IBM
Corp., 613 F.2d 727, 744 & n.29 (9th Cir. 1979) (memory).
Bundling can also capitalize on certain economies of scope. A
possible example is the "shared" library files that perform OS
and browser functions with the very same lines of code and
thus may save drive space from the clutter of redundant
routines and memory when consumers use both the OS and
browser simultaneously. 11/16/98 pm Tr. at 44 (trial testimony of Glenn Weadock), reprinted in 9 J.A. at 5892; Direct
Testimony of Microsoft's James Allchin p p 10, 97, 100, 106-

116, app. A (excluding p p f, g.vi), reprinted in 5 J.A. at 3292, 3322-30, 3412-17. Indeed, if there were no efficiencies from a tie (including economizing on consumer transaction costs such as the time and effort involved in choice), we would expect distinct consumer demand for each individual component of every good. In a competitive market with zero transaction costs, the computers on which this opinion was written would only be sold piecemeal--keyboard, monitor, mouse, central processing unit, disk drive, and memory all sold in separate transactions and likely by different manufacturers.

Recognizing the potential benefits from tying, see Jefferson Parish, 466 U.S. at 21 n.33, the Court in Jefferson Parish forged a separate-products test that, like those of market power and substantial foreclosure, attempts to screen out false positives under per se analysis. The consumer demand test is a rough proxy for whether a tying arrangement may, on balance, be welfare-enhancing, and unsuited to per se condemnation. In the abstract, of course, there is always direct separate demand for products: assuming choice is available at zero cost, consumers will prefer it to no choice. Only when the efficiencies from bundling are dominated by the benefits to choice for enough consumers, however, will we actually observe consumers making independent purchases. In other words, perceptible separate demand is inversely proportional to net efficiencies. On the supply side, firms without market power will bundle two goods only when the cost savings from joint sale outweigh the value consumers place on separate choice. So bundling by all competitive firms implies strong net efficiencies. If a court finds either that there is no noticeable separate demand for the tied product or, there being no convincing direct evidence of separate demand, that the entire "competitive fringe" engages in the same behavior as the defendant, 10 Areeda et al., Antitrust Law p 1744c4, at 200, then the tying and tied products should be declared one product and per se liability should be rejected.

Before concluding our exegesis of Jefferson Parish's separate-products test, we should clarify two things. First, Jefferson Parish does not endorse a direct inquiry into the

efficiencies of a bundle. Rather, it proposes easy-to-
administer proxies for net efficiency. In describing the separate-products test we discuss efficiencies only to explain the
rationale behind the consumer demand inquiry. To allow the
separate-products test to become a detailed inquiry into
possible welfare consequences would turn a screening test
into the very process it is expected to render unnecessary.
10 Areeda et al., Antitrust Law p p 1741b & c, at 180-85; see
also Jefferson Parish, 466 U.S. at 34-35 (O'Connor, J., concurring).

Second, the separate-products test is not a one-sided inquiry into the cost savings from a bundle. Although Jefferson
Parish acknowledged that prior lower court cases looked at
cost-savings to decide separate products, see id. at 22 n.35,
the Court conspicuously did not adopt that approach in its
disposition of tying arrangement before it. Instead it chose
proxies that balance costs savings against reduction in consumer choice.

With this background, we now turn to the separate-
products inquiry before us. The District Court found that
many consumers, if given the option, would choose their
browser separately from the OS. Findings of Fact p 151
(noting that "corporate consumers ... prefer to standardize
on the same browser across different [OSs]" at the work-
place). Turning to industry custom, the court found that,
although all major OS vendors bundled browsers with their
OSs, these companies either sold versions without a browser,
or allowed OEMs or end-users either not to install the
bundled browser or in any event to "uninstall" it. Id. p 153.
The court did not discuss the record evidence as to whether
OS vendors other than Microsoft sold at a bundled price, with
no discount for a browserless OS, perhaps because the record
evidence on the issue was in conflict. Compare, e.g., Direct
Testimony of Richard Schmalensee p 241, reprinted in 7 J.A.
at 4315 ("[A]ll major operating system vendors do in fact
include Web-browsing software with the operating system at
no extra charge.") (emphasis added), with, e.g., 1/6/99 pm Tr.
at 42 (trial testimony of Franklin Fisher of MIT) (suggesting
all OSs but Microsoft offer discounts).

Microsoft does not dispute that many consumers demand alternative browsers. But on industry custom Microsoft contends that no other firm requires non-removal because no other firm has invested the resources to integrate web browsing as deeply into its OS as Microsoft has. Appellant's Opening Br. at 25; cf. Direct Testimony of James Allchin p p 262-72, reprinted in 5 J.A. at 3385-89 (Apple, IBM); 11/5/98 pm Tr. at 55-58 (trial testimony of Apple's Avadis Tevanian, Jr.), reprinted in 9 J.A. at 5507-10 (Apple). (We here use the term "integrate" in the rather simple sense of converting individual goods into components of a single physical object (e.g., a computer as it leaves the OEM, or a disk or sets of disks), without any normative implication that such integration is desirable or achieves special advantages. Cf. United States v. Microsoft Corp., 147 F.3d 935, 950 (D.C. Cir. 1998) ("Microsoft II").) Microsoft contends not only that its integration of IE into Windows is innovative and beneficial but also that it requires non-removal of IE. In our discussion of monopoly maintenance we find that these claims fail the efficiency balancing applicable in that context. But the separate-products analysis is supposed to perform its function as a proxy without embarking on any direct analysis of efficiency. Accordingly, Microsoft's implicit argument--that in this case looking to a competitive fringe is inadequate to evaluate fully its potentially innovative technological integration, that such a comparison is between apples and oranges--poses a legitimate objection to the operation of Jefferson Parish's separate-products test for the per se rule.

In fact there is merit to Microsoft's broader argument that Jefferson Parish's consumer demand test would "chill innovation to the detriment of consumers by preventing firms from integrating into their products new functionality previously provided by standalone products--and hence, by definition, subject to separate consumer demand." Appellant's Opening Br. at 69. The per se rule's direct consumer demand and indirect industry custom inquiries are, as a general matter, backward-looking and therefore systematically poor proxies for overall efficiency in the presence of new and innovative integration. See 10 Areeda et al., Antitrust Law p 1746, at 224-29; Amicus Brief of Lawrence Lessig at 24-25, and sources cited therein (brief submitted regarding Conclusions of Law). The direct consumer demand test focuses on historic consumer behavior, likely before integration, and the indirect industry custom test looks at firms that, unlike the defendant, may not have integrated the tying and tied goods. Both tests compare incomparables--the defendant's decision to bundle in the presence of integration, on the one hand, and consumer and competitor calculations in its absence, on the other. If integration has efficiency benefits, these may be ignored by the Jefferson Parish proxies. Because one cannot be sure beneficial integration will be protected by the other elements of the per se rule, simple application of that rule's separate-products test may make consumers worse off.

In light of the monopoly maintenance section, obviously, we do not find that Microsoft's integration is welfare-enhancing or that it should be absolved of tying liability. Rather, we heed Microsoft's warning that the separate-products element of the per se rule may not give newly integrated products a fair shake.

B.   Per Se Analysis Inappropriate for this Case.

We now address directly the larger question as we see it: whether standard per se analysis should be applied "off the shelf" to evaluate the defendant's tying arrangement, one which involves software that serves as a platform for third-party applications. There is no doubt that "[i]t is far too late in the history of our antitrust jurisprudence to question the proposition that certain tying arrangements pose an unacceptable risk of stifling competition and therefore are unreasonable 'per se.' " Jefferson Parish, 466 U.S. at 9 (emphasis added). But there are strong reasons to doubt that the integration of additional software functionality into an OS falls among these arrangements. Applying per se analysis to

such an amalgamation creates undue risks of error and of
deterring welfare-enhancing innovation.

The Supreme Court has warned that " '[i]t is only after
considerable experience with certain business relationships
that courts classify them as per se violations....' " Broad.
Music, 441 U.S. at 9 (quoting Topco Assocs., 405 U.S. at 607-
08); accord Cont'l T.V., Inc. v. GTE Sylvania Inc., 433 U.S.
36, 47-59 (1977); White Motor Co. v. United States, 372 U.S.
253, 263 (1963); Jerrold Elecs., 187 F. Supp. at 555-58, 560-
61; see also Frank H. Easterbrook, Allocating Antitrust
Decisionmaking Tasks, 76 Geo. L.J. 305, 308 (1987). Yet the
sort of tying arrangement attacked here is unlike any the
Supreme Court has considered. The early Supreme Court
cases on tying dealt with arrangements whereby the sale or
lease of a patented product was conditioned on the purchase
of certain unpatented products from the patentee. See Motion Picture Patents, 243 U.S. 502 (1917); United Shoe
Mach., 258 U.S. 451 (1922); IBM Corp. v. United States, 298
U.S. 131 (1936); Int'l Salt, 332 U.S. 392 (1947). Later
Supreme Court tying cases did not involve market power
derived from patents, but continued to involve contractual
ties. See Times-Picayune, 345 U.S. 594 (1953) (defendant
newspaper conditioned the purchase of ads in its evening
edition on the purchase of ads in its morning edition); N. Pac.
Ry., 356 U.S. 1 (1958) (defendant railroad leased land only on
the condition that products manufactured on the land be
shipped on its railways); United States v. Loew's Inc., 371
U.S. 38 (1962) (defendant distributor of copyrighted feature
films conditioned the sale of desired films on the purchase of
undesired films); U.S. Steel Corp. v. Fortner Enters., Inc.,
429 U.S. 610 (1977) ("Fortner II") (defendant steel company
conditioned access to low interest loans on the purchase of the
defendant's prefabricated homes); Jefferson Parish, 466 U.S.
2 (1984) (defendant hospital conditioned use of its operating
rooms on the purchase of anesthesiological services from a
medical group associated with the hospital); Eastman Kodak,
504 U.S. 451 (1992) (defendant photocopying machine manufacturer conditioned the sale of replacement parts for its
machines on the use of the defendant's repair services).

In none of these cases was the tied good physically and
technologically integrated with the tying good. Nor did the
defendants ever argue that their tie improved the value of the
tying product to users and to makers of complementary
goods. In those cases where the defendant claimed that use
of the tied good made the tying good more valuable to users,
the Court ruled that the same result could be achieved via
quality standards for substitutes of the tied good. See, e.g.,
Int'l Salt, 332 U.S. at 397-98; IBM, 298 U.S. at 138-40.
Here Microsoft argues that IE and Windows are an integrated physical product and that the bundling of IE APIs with
Windows makes the latter a better applications platform for
third-party software. It is unclear how the benefits from IE
APIs could be achieved by quality standards for different
browser manufacturers. We do not pass judgment on Microsoft's claims regarding the benefits from integration of its
APIs. We merely note that these and other novel, purported
efficiencies suggest that judicial "experience" provides little
basis for believing that, "because of their pernicious effect on
competition and lack of any redeeming virtue," a software
firm's decisions to sell multiple functionalities as a package
should be "conclusively presumed to be unreasonable and
therefore illegal without elaborate inquiry as to the precise
harm they have caused or the business excuse for their use."
N. Pac. Ry., 356 U.S. at 5 (emphasis added).

     Nor have we found much insight into software integration
among the decisions of lower federal courts. Most tying
cases in the computer industry involve bundling with hardware. See, e.g., Digital Equip. Corp. v. Uniq Digital Techs.,
Inc., 73 F.3d 756, 761 (7th Cir. 1996) (Easterbrook, J.)
(rejecting with little discussion the notion that bundling of OS
with a computer is a tie of two separate products); Datagate,
Inc. v. Hewlett-Packard Co., 941 F.2d 864, 870 (9th Cir. 1991)
(holding that plaintiff's allegation that defendant conditioned
its software on purchase of its hardware was sufficient to
survive summary judgment); Digidyne Corp. v. Data Gen.
Corp., 734 F.2d 1336, 1341-47 (9th Cir. 1984) (holding that
defendant's conditioning the sale of its OS on the purchase of
its CPU constitutes a per se tying violation); Cal. Computer

Prods., 613 F.2d at 743-44 (holding that defendant's integration into its CPU of a disk controller designed for its own disk drives was a useful innovation and not an impermissible attempt to monopolize); ILC Peripherals Leasing Corp. v. IBM Corp., 448 F. Supp. 228, 233 (N.D. Cal. 1978) (finding that defendant's integration of magnetic disks and a head/disk assembly was not an unlawful tie), aff'd per curiam sub. nom. Memorex Corp. v. IBM Corp., 636 F.2d 1188 (9th Cir. 1980); see also Transamerica Computer Co. v. IBM Corp., 698 F.2d 1377, 1382-83 (9th Cir. 1983) (finding lawful defendant's design changes that rendered plaintiff peripheral maker's tape drives incompatible with the defendant's CPU). The hardware case that most resembles the present one is Telex Corp. v. IBM Corp., 367 F. Supp. 258 (N.D. Okla. 1973), rev'd on other grounds, 510 F.2d 894 (10th Cir. 1975). Just as Microsoft integrated web browsing into its OS, IBM in the 1970s integrated memory into its CPUs, a hardware platform. A peripheral manufacturer alleged a tying violation, but the District Court dismissed the claim because it thought it inappropriate to enmesh the courts in product design decisions. Id. at 347. The court's discussion of the tying claim was brief and did not dwell on the effects of the integration on competition or efficiencies. Nor did the court consider whether per se analysis of the alleged tie was wise.

We have found four antitrust cases involving arrangements in which a software program is tied to the purchase of a software platform--two district court cases and two appellate court cases, including one from this court. The first case, Innovation Data Processing, Inc. v. IBM Corp., 585 F. Supp. 1470 (D.N.J. 1984), involved an allegation that IBM bundled with its OS a utility used to transfer data from a tape drive to a computer's disk drive. Although the court mentioned the efficiencies achieved by bundling, it ultimately dismissed the per se tying claim because IBM sold a discounted version of the OS without the utility. Id. at 1475-76. The second case, A.I. Root Co. v. Computer/Dynamics, Inc., 806 F.2d 673 (6th Cir. 1986), was brought by a business customer who claimed that an OS manufacturer illegally conditioned the sale of its OS on the purchase of other software applications. The court

quickly disposed of the case on the ground that defendant
Computer/Dynamics had no market power. Id. at 675-77.
There was no mention of the efficiencies from the tie. The
third case, Caldera, Inc. v. Microsoft Corp., 72 F. Supp. 2d
1295 (D. Utah 1999), involved a complaint that the technological integration of MS-DOS and Windows 3.1 into Windows 95
constituted a per se tying violation. The court formulated the
"single product" issue in terms of whether the tie constituted
a technological improvement, ultimately concluding that Microsoft was not entitled to summary judgment on that issue.
Id. at 1322-28.

    The software case that bears the greatest resemblance to
that at bar is, not surprisingly, Microsoft II, 147 F.3d 935,
where we examined the bundling of IE with Windows 95.
But the issue there was whether the bundle constituted an
"integrated product" as the term was used in a 1994 consent
decree between the Department of Justice and Microsoft. Id.
at 939. We did not consider whether Microsoft's bundling
should be condemned as per se illegal. We certainly did not
make any finding that bundling IE with Windows had "no
purpose except stifling of competition," White Motor, 372 U.S.
at 263, an important consideration in defining the scope of
any of antitrust law's per se rules, see Cont'l T.V., 433 U.S. at
57-59. While we believed our interpretation of the term
"integrated product" was consistent with the test for separate
products under tying law, we made clear that the "antitrust
question is of course distinct." Microsoft II, 147 F.3d at 950
n.14. We even cautioned that our conclusion that IE and
Windows 95 were integrated was "subject to reexamination
on a more complete record." Id. at 952. To the extent that
the decision completely disclaimed judicial capacity to evaluate "high-tech product design," id., it cannot be said to
conform to prevailing antitrust doctrine (as opposed to resolution of the decree-interpretation issue then before us). In
any case, mere review of asserted breaches of a consent
decree hardly constitutes enough "experience" to warrant
application of per se analysis. See Broad. Music, 441 U.S. at
10-16 (refusing to apply per se analysis to defendant's blan-
ket licenses even though those licenses had been thoroughly

investigated by the Department of Justice and were the
subject of a consent decree that had been reviewed by
numerous courts).

While the paucity of cases examining software bundling
suggests a high risk that per se analysis may produce inaccu-
rate results, the nature of the platform software market
affirmatively suggests that per se rules might stunt valuable
innovation. We have in mind two reasons.

First, as we explained in the previous section, the separate-
products test is a poor proxy for net efficiency from newly
integrated products. Under per se analysis the first firm to
merge previously distinct functionalities (e.g., the inclusion of
starter motors in automobiles) or to eliminate entirely the
need for a second function (e.g., the invention of the stain-
resistant carpet) risks being condemned as having tied two
separate products because at the moment of integration there
will appear to be a robust "distinct" market for the tied
product. See 10 Areeda et al., Antitrust Law p 1746, at 224.
Rule of reason analysis, however, affords the first mover an
opportunity to demonstrate that an efficiency gain from its
"tie" adequately offsets any distortion of consumer choice.
See Grappone, Inc. v. Subaru of New England, Inc., 858 F.2d
792, 799 (1st Cir. 1988) (Breyer, J.); see also Town Sound &
Custom Tops, Inc. v. Chrysler Motor Corp., 959 F.2d 468, 482
(3d Cir. 1992); Kaiser Aluminum & Chem. Sales, Inc. v.
Avondale Shipyards, Inc., 677 F.2d 1045, 1048-49 n.5 (5th
Cir. 1982).

The failure of the separate-products test to screen out
certain cases of productive integration is particularly trou-
bling in platform software markets such as that in which the
defendant competes. Not only is integration common in such
markets, but it is common among firms without market
power. We have already reviewed evidence that nearly all
competitive OS vendors also bundle browsers. Moreover,
plaintiffs do not dispute that OS vendors can and do incorpo-
rate basic internet plumbing and other useful functionality
into their OSs. See Direct Testimony of Richard Schmalensee p 508, reprinted in 7 J.A. at 4462-64 (disk defragmenta-
tion, memory management, peer-to-peer networking or file
sharing); 11/19/98 am Tr. at 82-83 (trial testimony of Freder-

ick Warren-Boulton), reprinted in 10 J.A. at 6427-28
(TCP/IP stacks). Firms without market power have no incentive to package different pieces of software together unless there are efficiency gains from doing so. The ubiquity of
bundling in competitive platform software markets should
give courts reason to pause before condemning such behavior
in less competitive markets.

Second, because of the pervasively innovative character of
platform software markets, tying in such markets may produce efficiencies that courts have not previously encountered
and thus the Supreme Court had not factored into the per se
rule as originally conceived. For example, the bundling of a
browser with OSs enables an independent software developer
to count on the presence of the browser's APIs, if any, on
consumers' machines and thus to omit them from its own
package. See Direct Testimony of Richard Schmalensee
p p 230-31, 234, reprinted in 7 J.A. at 4309-11, 4312; Direct
Testimony of Michael Devlin p p 12-21, reprinted in 5 J.A. at
3525-29; see also Findings of Fact p 2. It is true that
software developers can bundle the browser APIs they need
with their own products, see id. p 193, but that may force
consumers to pay twice for the same API if it is bundled with
two different software programs. It is also true that OEMs
can include APIs with the computers they sell, id., but
diffusion of uniform APIs by that route may be inferior.
First, many OEMs serve special subsets of Windows consumers, such as home or corporate or academic users. If just one
of these OEMs decides not to bundle an API because it does
not benefit enough of its clients, ISVs that use that API
might have to bundle it with every copy of their program.
Second, there may be a substantial lag before all OEMs
bundle the same set of APIs--a lag inevitably aggravated by
the first phenomenon. In a field where programs change
very rapidly, delays in the spread of a necessary element
(here, the APIs) may be very costly. Of course, these
arguments may not justify Microsoft's decision to bundle
APIs in this case, particularly because Microsoft did not
merely bundle with Windows the APIs from IE, but an entire
browser application (sometimes even without APIs, see id.).

A justification for bundling a component of software may not be one for bundling the entire software package, especially given the malleability of software code. See id. p p 162-63; 12/9/98 am Tr. at 17 (trial testimony of David Farber); 1/6/99 am Tr. at 6-7 (trial testimony of Franklin Fisher), reprinted in 11 J.A. at 7192-93; Direct Testimony of Joachim Kempin p 286, reprinted in 6 J.A. at 3749. Furthermore, the interest in efficient API diffusion obviously supplies a far stronger justification for simple price-bundling than for Microsoft's contractual or technological bars to subsequent removal of functionality. But our qualms about redefining the boundaries of a defendant's product and the possibility of consumer gains from simplifying the work of applications developers makes us question any hard and fast approach to tying in OS software markets.

There may also be a number of efficiencies that, although very real, have been ignored in the calculations underlying the adoption of a per se rule for tying. We fear that these efficiencies are common in technologically dynamic markets where product development is especially unlikely to follow an easily foreseen linear pattern. Take the following example from ILC Peripherals, 448 F. Supp. 228, a case concerning the evolution of disk drives for computers. When IBM first introduced such drives in 1956, it sold an integrated product that contained magnetic disks and disk heads that read and wrote data onto disks. Id. at 231. Consumers of the drives demanded two functions--to store data and to access it all at once. In the first few years consumers' demand for storage increased rapidly, outpacing the evolution of magnetic disk technology. To satisfy that demand IBM made it possible for consumers to remove the magnetic disks from drives, even though that meant consumers would not have access to data on disks removed from the drive. This componentization enabled makers of computer peripherals to sell consumers removable disks. Id. at 231-32. Over time, however, the technology of magnetic disks caught up with demand for capacity, so that consumers needed few removable disks to store all their data. At this point IBM reintegrated disks into their drives, enabling consumers to once again have

immediate access to all their data without a sacrifice in
capacity. Id. A manufacturer of removable disks sued. But
the District Court found the tie justified because it satisfied
consumer demand for immediate access to all data, and ruled
that disks and disk heads were one product. Id. at 233. A
court hewing more closely to the truncated analysis contem-
plated by Northern Pacific Railway would perhaps have
overlooked these consumer benefits.

These arguments all point to one conclusion: we cannot
comfortably say that bundling in platform software markets
has so little "redeeming virtue," N. Pac. Ry., 356 U.S. at 5,
and that there would be so "very little loss to society" from
its ban, that "an inquiry into its costs in the individual case
[can be] considered [ ] unnecessary." Jefferson Parish, 466
U.S. at 33-34 (O'Connor, J., concurring). We do not have
enough empirical evidence regarding the effect of Microsoft's
practice on the amount of consumer surplus created or consumer choice foreclosed by the integration of added functionality into platform software to exercise sensible judgment
regarding that entire class of behavior. (For some issues we
have no data.) "We need to know more than we do about the
actual impact of these arrangements on competition to decide
whether they ... should be classified as per se violations of
the Sherman Act." White Motor, 372 U.S. at 263. Until
then, we will heed the wisdom that "easy labels do not always
supply ready answers," Broad. Music, 441 U.S. at 8, and
vacate the District Court's finding of per se tying liability
under Sherman Act s 1. We remand the case for evaluation
of Microsoft's tying arrangements under the rule of reason.
See Pullman-Standard v. Swint, 456 U.S. 273, 292 (1982)
("[W]here findings are infirm because of an erroneous view of
the law, a remand is the proper course unless the record
permits only one resolution of the factual issue."). That rule
more freely permits consideration of the benefits of bundling
in software markets, particularly those for OSs, and a balancing of these benefits against the costs to consumers whose
ability to make direct price/quality tradeoffs in the tied
market may have been impaired. See Jefferson Parish, 466
U.S. at 25 nn.41-42 (noting that per se rule does not broadly

permit consideration of procompetitive justifications); id. at
34-35 (O'Connor, J., concurring); N. Pac. Ry., 356 U.S. at 5.

Our judgment regarding the comparative merits of the per
se rule and the rule of reason is confined to the tying
arrangement before us, where the tying product is software
whose major purpose is to serve as a platform for third-party
applications and the tied product is complementary software
functionality. While our reasoning may at times appear to
have broader force, we do not have the confidence to speak to
facts outside the record, which contains scant discussion of
software integration generally. Microsoft's primary justification for bundling IE APIs is that their inclusion with Windows increases the value of third-party software (and Windows) to consumers. See Appellant's Opening Br. at 41-43.
Because this claim applies with distinct force when the tying
product is platform software, we have no present basis for
finding the per se rule inapplicable to software markets
generally. Nor should we be interpreted as setting a prece-
dent for switching to the rule of reason every time a court
identifies an efficiency justification for a tying arrangement.
Our reading of the record suggests merely that integration of
new functionality into platform software is a common practice
and that wooden application of per se rules in this litigation
may cast a cloud over platform innovation in the market for
PCs, network computers and information appliances.

C.   On Remand

Should plaintiffs choose to pursue a tying claim under the
rule of reason, we note the following for the benefit of the
trial court:

First, on remand, plaintiffs must show that Microsoft's
conduct unreasonably restrained competition. Meeting that
burden "involves an inquiry into the actual effect" of Microsoft's conduct on competition in the tied good market, Jefferson Parish, 466 U.S. at 29, the putative market for browsers.
To the extent that certain aspects of tying injury may depend
on a careful definition of the tied good market and a showing
of barriers to entry other than the tying arrangement itself,

plaintiffs would have to establish these points. See Jefferson
Parish, 466 U.S. at 29 ("This competition [among anesthesiol-
ogists] takes place in a market that has not been defined.");
id. at 29 n.48 ("[N]either the District Court nor the Court of
Appeals made any findings concerning the contract's effect on
entry barriers."). But plaintiffs were required--and had
every incentive--to provide both a definition of the browser
market and barriers to entry to that market as part of their
s 2 attempted monopolization claim; yet they failed to do so.
See supra Section III. Accordingly, on remand of the s 1
tying claim, plaintiffs will be precluded from arguing any
theory of harm that depends on a precise definition of browsers or barriers to entry (for example, network effects from
Internet protocols and extensions embedded in a browser)
other than what may be implicit in Microsoft's tying arrangement.

     Of the harms left, plaintiffs must show that Microsoft's
conduct was, on balance, anticompetitive. Microsoft may of
course offer procompetitive justifications, and it is plaintiffs'
burden to show that the anticompetitive effect of the conduct
outweighs its benefit.

     Second, the fact that we have already considered some of
the behavior plaintiffs allege to constitute tying violations in
the monopoly maintenance section does not resolve the s 1
inquiry. The two practices that plaintiffs have most ardently
claimed as tying violations are, indeed, a basis for liability
under plaintiffs' s 2 monopoly maintenance claim. These are
Microsoft's refusal to allow OEMs to uninstall IE or remove
it from the Windows desktop, Findings of Fact p p 158, 203,
213, and its removal of the IE entry from the Add/Remove
Programs utility in Windows 98, id. p 170. See supra Section
II.B. In order for the District Court to conclude these
practices also constitute s 1 tying violations, plaintiffs must
demonstrate that their benefits--if any, see supra Sections
II.B.1.b and II.B.2.b; Findings of Fact p p 176, 186, 193--are
outweighed by the harms in the tied product market. See
Jefferson Parish, 466 U.S. at 29. If the District Court is
convinced of net harm, it must then consider whether any
additional remedy is necessary.

In Section II.B we also considered another alleged tying violation--the Windows 98 override of a consumer's choice of default web browser. We concluded that this behavior does not provide a distinct basis for s 2 liability because plaintiffs failed to rebut Microsoft's proffered justification by demonstrating that harms in the operating system market outweigh Microsoft's claimed benefits. See supra Section II.B. On remand, however, although Microsoft may offer the same procompetitive justification for the override, plaintiffs must have a new opportunity to rebut this claim, by demonstrating that the anticompetitive effect in the browser market is greater than these benefits.

Finally, the District Court must also consider an alleged tying violation that we did not consider under s 2 monopoly maintenance: price bundling. First, the court must determine if Microsoft indeed price bundled--that is, was Microsoft's charge for Windows and IE higher than its charge would have been for Windows alone? This will require plaintiffs to resolve the tension between Findings of Fact p p 136-37, which Microsoft interprets as saying that no part of the bundled price of Windows can be attributed to IE, and Conclusions of Law, at 50, which says the opposite. Compare Direct Testimony of Paul Maritz p p 37, 296, reprinted in 6 J.A. at 3656, 3753-54 (Microsoft did not "charge separately" for IE, but like all other major OS vendors included browsing software at "no extra charge"), with GX 202 at MS7 004343, esp. 004347, reprinted in 22 J.A. at 14459, esp. 14463 (memo from Christian Wildfeuer describing focus group test used to price Windows 98 with IE 4), and GX 1371 at MS7 003729-30, 003746, 003748, esp. 003750, reprinted in 15 J.A. at 10306-07, 10323, 10325, esp. 10327 (Windows 98 pricing and marketing memo), and Findings of Fact p 63 (identifying GX 202 as the basis for Windows 98 pricing).

If there is a positive price increment in Windows associated with IE (we know there is no claim of price predation), plaintiffs must demonstrate that the anticompetitive effects of Microsoft's price bundling outweigh any procompetitive justifications the company provides for it. In striking this balance, the District Court should consider, among other things, indirect evidence of efficiency provided by "the competitive fringe." See supra Section IV.A. Although this inquiry may overlap with the separate-products screen under the per se rule, that is not its role here. Because courts applying the rule of reason are free to look at both direct and indirect evidence of efficiencies from a tie, there is no need for a screening device as such; thus the separate-products inquiry serves merely to classify arrangements as subject to tying law, as opposed to, say, liability for exclusive dealing. See Times-Picayune, 345 U.S. at 614 (finding a single product and then turning to a general rule of reason analysis under s 1, though not using the term "tying"); Foster v. Md. State Sav. & Loan Ass'n, 590 F.2d 928, 931, 933 (D.C. Cir. 1978), cited in Jefferson Parish, 466 U.S. at 40 (O'Connor, J., concurring) (same); see also Chawla v. Shell Oil Co., 75 F. Supp. 2d 626, 635, 643-44 (S.D. Tex. 1999) (considering a rule of reason tying claim after finding a single product under the per se rule); Montgomery County Ass'n of Realtors v. Realty Photo Master Corp., 783 F. Supp. 952, 961 & n.26 (D. Md. 1992), aff'd mem. 993 F.2d 1538 (4th Cir. 1993) (same).

If OS vendors without market power also sell their software bundled with a browser, the natural inference is that sale of the items as a bundle serves consumer demand and that unbundled sale would not, for otherwise a competitor could profitably offer the two products separately and capture sales of the tying good from vendors that bundle. See 10 Areeda et al., Antitrust Law p 1744b, at 197-98. It does appear that most if not all firms have sold a browser with their OSs at a bundled price, beginning with IBM and its OS/2 Warp OS in September 1994, Findings of Fact p 140; see also Direct Testimony of Richard Schmalensee p 212, reprinted in 7 J.A. at 4300-01, and running to current versions of Apple's Mac OS, Caldera and Red Hat's Linux OS, Sun's Solaris OS, Be's BeOS, Santa Cruz Operation's UnixWare, Novell's NetWare OS, and others, see Findings of Fact p 153; Direct Testimony of Richard Schmalensee p p 215-23, 230, esp. table 5, reprinted in 7 J.A. at 4302-05,

4310; Direct Testimony of James Allchin p p 261-77, reprinted in 5 J.A. at 3384-92.

Of course price bundling by competitive OS makers would
tend to exonerate Microsoft only if the sellers in question sold
their browser/OS combinations exclusively at a bundled price.
If a competitive seller offers a discount for a browserless
version, then--at least as to its OS and browser--the gains
from bundling are outweighed by those from separate choice.
The evidence on discounts appears to be in conflict. Compare
Direct Testimony of Richard Schmalensee p 241, reprinted in
7 J.A. at 4315, with 1/6/99 pm Tr. at 42 (trial testimony of
Franklin Fisher). If Schmalensee is correct that nearly all
OS makers do not offer a discount, then the harm from
tying--obstruction of direct consumer choice--would be theo-
retically created by virtually all sellers: a customer who
would prefer an alternate browser is forced to pay the full
price of that browser even though its value to him is only the
increment in value over the bundled browser. (The result is
similar to that from non-removal, which forces consumers
who want the alternate browser to surrender disk space
taken up by the unused, bundled browser.) If the failure to
offer a price discount were universal, any impediment to
direct consumer choice created by Microsoft's price-bundled
sale of IE with Windows would be matched throughout the
market; yet these OS suppliers on the competitive fringe
would have evidently found this price bundling on balance
efficient. If Schmalensee's assertions are ill-founded, of
course, no such inference could be drawn.

V. Trial Proceedings and Remedy

Microsoft additionally challenges the District Court's procedural rulings on two fronts. First, with respect to the trial
phase, Microsoft proposes that the court mismanaged its
docket by adopting an expedited trial schedule and receiving
evidence through summary witnesses. Second, with respect
to the remedies decree, Microsoft argues that the court
improperly ordered that it be divided into two separate
companies. Only the latter claim will long detain us. The
District Court's trial-phase procedures were comfortably
within the bounds of its broad discretion to conduct trials as it
sees fit. We conclude, however, that the District Court's

remedies decree must be vacated for three independent reasons: (1) the court failed to hold a remedies-specific evidentiary hearing when there were disputed facts; (2) the court failed to provide adequate reasons for its decreed remedies; and (3) this Court has revised the scope of Microsoft's liability and it is impossible to determine to what extent that should affect the remedies provisions.

A.   Factual Background

On April 3, 2000, the District Court concluded the liability phase of the proceedings by the filing of its Conclusions of Law holding that Microsoft had violated ss 1 and 2 of the Sherman Act. The court and the parties then began discussions of the procedures to be followed in the imposition of remedies. Initially, the District Court signaled that it would enter relief only after conducting a new round of proceedings. In its Conclusions of Law, the court stated that it would issue a remedies order "following proceedings to be established by further Order of the Court." Conclusions of Law, at 57. And, when during a post-trial conference, Microsoft's counsel asked whether the court "contemplate[d] further proceedings," the judge replied, "Yes. Yes. I assume that there would be further proceedings." 4/4/00 Tr. at 8-9, 11, reprinted in 4 J.A. at 2445-46, 2448. The District Court further speculated that those proceedings might "replicate the procedure at trial with testimony in written form subject to cross-examination." Id. at 11, reprinted in 4 J.A. at 2448.

On April 28, 2000, plaintiffs submitted their proposed final judgment, accompanied by six new supporting affidavits and several exhibits. In addition to a series of temporary conduct restrictions, plaintiffs proposed that Microsoft be split into two independent corporations, with one continuing Microsoft's operating systems business and the other undertaking the balance of Microsoft's operations. Plaintiffs' Proposed Final Judgment at 2-3, reprinted in 4 J.A. at 2473-74. Microsoft filed a "summary response" on May 10, contending both that the proposed decree was too severe and that it would be impossible to resolve certain remedies-specific factual disputes "on a highly expedited basis." Defendant's Summary

Response at 6-7, reprinted in 4 J.A. at 2587-88. Another May 10 submission argued that if the District Court considered imposing plaintiffs' proposed remedy, "then substantial discovery, adequate time for preparation and a full trial on relief will be required." Defendant's Position as to Future Proceedings at 2, reprinted in 4 J.A. at 2646.

After the District Court revealed during a May 24 hearing that it was prepared to enter a decree without conducting "any further process," 5/24/00 pm Tr. at 33, reprinted in 14 J.A. at 9866, Microsoft renewed its argument that the underlying factual disputes between the parties necessitated a remedies-specific evidentiary hearing. In two separate offers of proof, Microsoft offered to produce a number of pieces of evidence, including the following:

- Testimony from Dr. Robert Crandall, a Senior Fellow at the Brookings Institution, that divestiture and dissolution orders historically have "failed to improve economic welfare by reducing prices or increasing output." Defendant's Offer of Proof at 2, reprinted in 4 J.A. at 2743.

- Testimony from Professor Kenneth Elzinga, Professor of Economics at the University of Virginia, that plaintiffs' proposed remedies would not induce entry into the operating systems market. Id. at 4, reprinted in 4 J.A. at 2745.

- Testimony from Dean Richard Schmalensee, Dean of MIT's Sloan School of Management, that dividing Microsoft likely would "harm consumers through higher prices, lower output, reduced efficiency, and less innovation" and would "produce immediate, substantial increases in the prices of both Windows and Office." Id. at 8, reprinted in 4 J.A. at 2749. Indeed, it would cause the price of Windows to triple. Id.

- Testimony from Goldman, Sachs & Co. and from Morgan Stanley Dean Witter that dissolution would adversely affect shareholder value. Id. at 17, 19, reprinted in 4 J.A. at 2758, 2760.

.   Testimony from Microsoft Chairman Bill Gates that
    dividing Microsoft "along the arbitrary lines proposed
    by the Government" would devastate the company's
    proposed Next Generation Windows Services plat-
    form, which would allow software developers to write
    web-based applications that users could access from a
    wide range of devices. Id. at 21-22, reprinted in 4
    J.A. at 2762-63.

.   Testimony from Steve Ballmer, Microsoft's President
    and CEO, that Microsoft is organized as a unified
    company and that "there are no natural lines along
    which Microsoft could be broken up without causing
    serious problems." Id. at 23, reprinted in 4 J.A. at
    2764.

.   Testimony from Michael Capellas, CEO of Compaq,
    that splitting Microsoft in two "will make it more
    difficult for OEMs to provide customers with the
    tightly integrated product offerings they demand" in
    part because "complementary products created by
    unrelated companies do not work as well together as
    products created by a single company." Defendant's
    Supplemental Offer of Proof at 2, reprinted in 4 J.A.
    at 2823.

Over Microsoft's objections, the District Court proceeded to
consider the merits of the remedy and on June 7, 2000
entered its final judgment. The court explained that it would
not conduct "extended proceedings on the form a remedy
should take," because it doubted that an evidentiary hearing
would "give any significantly greater assurance that it will be
able to identify what might be generally regarded as an
optimum remedy." Final Judgment, at 62. The bulk of
Microsoft's proffered facts were simply conjectures about
future events, and "[i]n its experience the Court has found
testimonial predictions of future events generally less reliable
even than testimony as to historical fact, and cross-
examination to be of little use in enhancing or detracting from
their accuracy." Id. Nor was the court swayed by Microsoft's "profession of surprise" at the possibility of structural
relief. Id. at 61. "From the inception of this case Microsoft

knew, from well-established Supreme Court precedents dat-
ing from the beginning of the last century, that a mandated
divestiture was a possibility, if not a probability, in the event
of an adverse result at trial." Id.

The substance of the District Court's remedies order is
nearly identical to plaintiffs' proposal. The decree's center-
piece is the requirement that Microsoft submit a proposed
plan of divestiture, with the company to be split into an
"Operating Systems Business," or "OpsCo," and an "Applications Business," or "AppsCo." Final Judgment, Decree
ss 1.a, 1.c.i, at 64. OpsCo would receive all of Microsoft's
operating systems, such as Windows 98 and Windows 2000,
while AppsCo would receive the remainder of Microsoft's
businesses, including IE and Office. The District Court
identified four reasons for its "reluctant[ ]" conclusion that "a
structural remedy has become imperative." Id. at 62. First,
Microsoft "does not yet concede that any of its business
practices violated the Sherman Act." Id. Second, the company consequently "continues to do business as it has in the
past." Id. Third, Microsoft "has proved untrustworthy in
the past." Id. And fourth, the Government, whose officials
"are by reason of office obliged and expected to consider--
and to act in--the public interest," won the case, "and for that
reason alone have some entitlement to a remedy of their
choice." Id. at 62-63.

The decree also contains a number of interim restrictions
on Microsoft's conduct. For instance, Decree s 3.b requires
Microsoft to disclose to third-party developers the APIs and
other technical information necessary to ensure that software
effectively interoperates with Windows. Id. at 67. "To facili-
tate compliance," s 3.b further requires that Microsoft establish "a secure facility" at which third-party representatives
may "study, interrogate and interact with relevant and necessary portions of [Microsoft platform software] source code."
Id. Section 3.e, entitled "Ban on Exclusive Dealing," forbids
Microsoft from entering contracts which oblige third parties
to restrict their "development, production, distribution, promotion or use of, or payment for" non-Microsoft platform-
level software. Id. at 68. Under Decree s 3.f--"Ban on

Contractual Tying"--the company may not condition its grant
of a Windows license on a party's agreement "to license,
promote, or distribute any other Microsoft software product."
Id. And s 3.g imposes a "Restriction on Binding Middleware
Products to Operating System Products" unless Microsoft
also offers consumers "an otherwise identical version" of the
operating system without the middleware. Id.

B.   Trial Proceedings

     Microsoft's first contention--that the District Court erred
by adopting an expedited trial schedule and receiving evidence through summary witnesses--is easily disposed of.
Trial courts have extraordinarily broad discretion to determine the manner in which they will conduct trials. "This is
particularly true in a case such as the one at bar where the
proceedings are being tried to the court without a jury." Eli
Lilly & Co., Inc. v. Generix Drug Sales, Inc., 460 F.2d 1096,
1105 (5th Cir. 1972). In such cases, "[a]n appellate court will
not interfere with the trial court's exercise of its discretion to
control its docket and dispatch its business ... except upon
the clearest showing that the procedures have resulted in
actual and substantial prejudice to the complaining litigant."
Id. Microsoft fails to clear this high hurdle. Although the
company claims that setting an early trial date inhibited its
ability to conduct discovery, it never identified a specific
deposition or document it was unable to obtain. And while
Microsoft now argues that the use of summary witnesses
made inevitable the improper introduction of hearsay evidence, the company actually agreed to the District Court's
proposal to limit each side to 12 summary witnesses. 12/2/98
am Tr. at 11, reprinted in 21 J.A. at 14083 (court admonish-
ing Microsoft's counsel to "[k]eep in mind that both sides
agreed to the number of witnesses"). Even absent Microsoft's agreement, the company's challenge fails to show that
this use of summary witnesses falls outside the trial court's
wide latitude to receive evidence as it sees fit. General Elec.
Co. v. Joiner, 522 U.S. 136, 141-42 (1997). This is particularly true given the presumption that a judge who conducts a
bench trial has ignored any inadmissible evidence, Harris v.
Rivera, 454 U.S. 339, 346 (1981)--a presumption that Micro-

soft makes no serious attempt to overcome. Indeed, under
appropriate circumstances with appropriate instructions, we
have in the past approved the use of summary witnesses even
in jury trials. See, e.g., United States v. Lemire, 720 F.2d
1327 (D.C. Cir. 1983). Therefore, neither the use of the
summary witnesses nor any other aspect of the District
Court's conduct of the trial phase amounted to an abuse of
discretion.

C.   Failure to Hold an Evidentiary Hearing

     The District Court's remedies-phase proceedings are a
different matter. It is a cardinal principle of our system of
justice that factual disputes must be heard in open court and
resolved through trial-like evidentiary proceedings. Any other course would be contrary "to the spirit which imbues our
judicial tribunals prohibiting decision without hearing." Sims
v. Greene, 161 F.2d 87, 88 (3d Cir. 1947).

     A party has the right to judicial resolution of disputed facts
not just as to the liability phase, but also as to appropriate
relief. "Normally, an evidentiary hearing is required before
an injunction may be granted." United States v. McGee, 714
F.2d 607, 613 (6th Cir. 1983); see also Charlton v. Estate of
Charlton, 841 F.2d 988, 989 (9th Cir. 1988) ("Generally the
entry or continuation of an injunction requires a hearing.
Only when the facts are not in dispute, or when the adverse
party has waived its right to a hearing, can that significant
procedural step be eliminated." (citation and internal quota-
tion marks omitted)). Other than a temporary restraining
order, no injunctive relief may be entered without a hearing.
See generally Fed. R. Civ. P. 65. A hearing on the merits--
i.e., a trial on liability--does not substitute for a relief-specific
evidentiary hearing unless the matter of relief was part of the
trial on liability, or unless there are no disputed factual issues
regarding the matter of relief.

     This rule is no less applicable in antitrust cases. The
Supreme Court "has recognized that a 'full exploration of
facts is usually necessary in order (for the District Court)
properly to draw (an antitrust) decree' so as 'to prevent
future violations and eradicate existing evils.' " United States

v. Ward Baking Co., 376 U.S. 327, 330-31 (1964) (quoting
Associated Press v. United States, 326 U.S. 1, 22 (1945)).
Hence a remedies decree must be vacated whenever there is
"a bona fide disagreement concerning substantive items of
relief which could be resolved only by trial." Id. at 334; cf.
Sims, 161 F.2d at 89 ("It has never been supposed that a
temporary injunction could issue under the Clayton Act without giving the party against whom the injunction was sought
an opportunity to present evidence on his behalf.").

        Despite plaintiffs' protestations, there can be no serious
doubt that the parties disputed a number of facts during the
remedies phase. In two separate offers of proof, Microsoft
identified 23 witnesses who, had they been permitted to
testify, would have challenged a wide range of plaintiffs'
factual representations, including the feasibility of dividing
Microsoft, the likely impact on consumers, and the effect of
divestiture on shareholders. To take but two examples,
where plaintiffs' economists testified that splitting Microsoft
in two would be socially beneficial, the company offered to
prove that the proposed remedy would "cause substantial
social harm by raising software prices, lowering rates of
innovation and disrupting the evolution of Windows as a
software development platform." Defendant's Offer of Proof
at 6, reprinted in 4 J.A. at 2747. And where plaintiffs'
investment banking experts proposed that divestiture might
actually increase shareholder value, Microsoft proffered evidence that structural relief "would inevitably result in a
significant loss of shareholder value," a loss that could reach
"tens--possibly hundreds--of billions of dollars." Id. at 19,
reprinted in 4 J.A. at 2760.

        Indeed, the District Court itself appears to have conceded
the existence of acute factual disagreements between Microsoft and plaintiffs. The court acknowledged that the parties
were "sharply divided" and held "divergent opinions" on the
likely results of its remedies decree. Final Judgment, at 62.
The reason the court declined to conduct an evidentiary
hearing was not because of the absence of disputed facts, but
because it believed that those disputes could be resolved only
through "actual experience," not further proceedings. Id.

But a prediction about future events is not, as a prediction, any less a factual issue. Indeed, the Supreme Court has acknowledged that drafting an antitrust decree by necessity "involves predictions and assumptions concerning future economic and business events." Ford Motor Co. v. United States, 405 U.S. 562, 578 (1972). Trial courts are not excused from their obligation to resolve such matters through evidentiary hearings simply because they consider the bedrock procedures of our justice system to be "of little use." Final Judgment, at 62.

The presence of factual disputes thus distinguishes this case from the decisions plaintiffs cite for the proposition that Microsoft was not entitled to an evidentiary hearing. Indeed, far from assisting plaintiffs, these cases actually confirm the proposition that courts must hold evidentiary hearings when they are confronted with disputed facts. In Ford Motor Co., the Supreme Court affirmed a divestiture order after emphasizing that the District Court had "held nine days of hearings on the remedy." 405 U.S. at 571. In Davoll v. Webb, 194 F.3d 1116 (10th Cir. 1999), the defendant both failed to submit any offers of proof, and waived its right to an evidentiary hearing by expressly agreeing that relief should be determined based solely on written submissions. Id. at 1142-43. The defendants in American Can Co. v. Mansukhani, 814 F.2d 421 (7th Cir. 1987), were not entitled to a hearing on remedies because they failed "to explain to the district court what new proof they would present to show" that the proposed remedy was unwarranted. Id. at 425. And in Socialist Workers Party v. Illinois State Board of Elections, 566 F.2d 586 (7th Cir. 1977), aff'd, 440 U.S. 173 (1979), the Seventh Circuit held that a remedies-specific hearing was unnecessary because that case involved a pure question of legal interpretation and hence "[t]here was no factual dispute as to the ground on which the injunction was ordered." Id. at 587.

Unlike the parties in Davoll, American Can, and Socialist Workers Party, Microsoft both repeatedly asserted its right to an evidentiary hearing and submitted two offers of proof. The company's "summary response" to the proposed remedy argued that it would be "impossible" to address underlying

factual issues "on a highly expedited basis," Defendant's
Summary Response at 6-7, reprinted in 4 J.A. at 2587-88,
and Microsoft further maintained that the court could not
issue a decree unless it first permitted "substantial discovery,
adequate time for preparation and a full trial on relief."
Defendant's Position as to Future Proceedings at 2, reprinted
in 4 J.A. at 2646. And in 53 pages of submissions, Microsoft
identified the specific evidence it would introduce to challenge
plaintiffs' representations.

Plaintiffs further argue--and the District Court held--that
no evidentiary hearing was necessary given that Microsoft
long had been on notice that structural relief was a distinct
possibility. It is difficult to see why this matters. Whether
Microsoft had advance notice that dissolution was in the
works is immaterial to whether the District Court violated the
company's procedural rights by ordering it without an evidentiary hearing. To be sure, "claimed surprise at the district
court's decision to consider permanent injunctive relief does
not, alone, merit reversal." Socialist Workers, 566 F.2d at
587. But in this case, Microsoft's professed surprise does not
stand "alone." There is something more: the company's
basic procedural right to have disputed facts resolved through
an evidentiary hearing.

In sum, the District Court erred when it resolved the
parties' remedies-phase factual disputes by consulting only
the evidence introduced during trial and plaintiffs' remedies-
phase submissions, without considering the evidence Microsoft sought to introduce. We therefore vacate the District
Court's final judgment, and remand with instructions to conduct a remedies-specific evidentiary hearing.

D.   Failure to Provide an Adequate Explanation

We vacate the District Court's remedies decree for the
additional reason that the court has failed to provide an
adequate explanation for the relief it ordered. The Supreme
Court has explained that a remedies decree in an antitrust
case must seek to "unfetter a market from anticompetitive
conduct," Ford Motor Co., 405 U.S. at 577, to "terminate the
illegal monopoly, deny to the defendant the fruits of its

statutory violation, and ensure that there remain no practices
likely to result in monopolization in the future," United States
v. United Shoe Mach. Corp., 391 U.S. 244, 250 (1968); see
also United States v. Grinnell Corp., 384 U.S. 563, 577 (1966).

The District Court has not explained how its remedies
decree would accomplish those objectives. Indeed, the court
devoted a mere four paragraphs of its order to explaining its
reasons for the remedy. They are: (1) Microsoft "does not
yet concede that any of its business practices violated the
Sherman Act"; (2) Microsoft "continues to do business as it
has in the past"; (3) Microsoft "has proved untrustworthy in
the past"; and (4) the Government, whose officials "are by
reason of office obliged and expected to consider--and to act
in--the public interest," won the case, "and for that reason
alone have some entitlement to a remedy of their choice."
Final Judgment, at 62-63. Nowhere did the District Court
discuss the objectives the Supreme Court deems relevant.

E.   Modification of Liability

Quite apart from its procedural difficulties, we vacate the
District Court's final judgment in its entirety for the additional, independent reason that we have modified the underlying
bases of liability. Of the three antitrust violations originally
identified by the District Court, one is no longer viable:
attempted monopolization of the browser market in violation
of Sherman Act s 2. One will be remanded for liability
proceedings under a different legal standard: unlawful tying
in violation of s 1. Only liability for the s 2 monopoly-
maintenance violation has been affirmed--and even that we
have revised. Ordinarily, of course, we review the grant or
denial of equitable relief under the abuse of discretion standard. See, e.g., Doran v. Salem Inn, Inc., 422 U.S. 922, 931-
32 (1975) ("[T]he standard of appellate review is simply
whether the issuance of the injunction, in the light of the
applicable standard, constituted an abuse of discretion.").
For obvious reasons, the application of that standard is not
sufficient to sustain the remedy in the case before us. We
cannot determine whether the District Court has abused its
discretion in remedying a wrong where the court did not

exercise that discretion in order to remedy the properly
determined wrong. That is, the District Court determined
that the conduct restrictions and the pervasive structural
remedy were together appropriate to remedy the three antitrust violations set forth above. The court did not exercise
its discretion to determine whether all, or for that matter,
any, of those equitable remedies were required to rectify a
s 2 monopoly maintenance violation taken alone. We therefore cannot sustain an exercise of discretion not yet made.

By way of comparison, in Spectrum Sports, Inc. v. McQuillan, 506 U.S. 447 (1993), the Supreme Court reviewed a
damages award in a Sherman Act case. In that case, the trial
court entered judgment upon a jury verdict which did not
differentiate among multiple possible theories of liability under s 2. The Supreme Court ultimately determined that the
trial record could not legally support a finding that the
defendant had committed an illegal attempt to monopolize,
and that "the trial instructions allowed the jury to infer
specific intent and dangerous probability of success from the
defendants' predatory conduct, without any proof of the relevant market or of a realistic probability that the defendants
could achieve monopoly power in that market." Id. at 459.
Therefore, the High Court reversed the Ninth Circuit's judgment affirming the District Court and remanded for further
proceedings, expressly because "the jury's verdict did not
negate the possibility that the s 2 verdict rested on the
attempt to monopolize grounds alone...." Id. Similarly,
here, we cannot presume that a District Court would exercise
its discretion to fashion the same remedy where the erroneous grounds of liability were stripped from its consideration.

The Eighth Circuit confronted a similar problem in Con-
cord Boat Corp. v. Brunswick Corp., 207 F.3d 1039 (8th Cir.),
cert. denied, 121 S. Ct. 428 (2000). In that case, a group of
boat builders brought an action against an engine manufacturer alleging violations of Sherman Act ss 1 and 2, and
Clayton Act s 7. After a 10-week trial, the jury found
Brunswick liable on all three counts and returned a verdict
for over $44 million. On appeal, the Eighth Circuit reversed
the Clayton Act claim. Id. at 1053. That court held that, as

a consequence, it was required to vacate the jury's remedy in
its entirety. Because the "verdict form did not require the
jury to consider what damages resulted from each type of
violation," the court could not "know what damages it found
to have been caused by the acquisitions upon which the
Section 7 claims were based." Id. at 1054. The court
rejected the proposition that "the entire damage award may
be upheld based on Brunswick's Sherman Act liability alone,"
id. at 1053, holding that, because "there is no way to know
what damages the jury assigned to the Section 7 claims," the
defendant "would be entitled at the very least to a new
damages trial on the boat builders' Sherman Act claims," id.
at 1054.

     Spectrum Sports and Concord Boat are distinguishable
from the case before us in that both involved the award of
money damages rather than equitable relief. Nonetheless,
their reasoning is instructive. A court in both contexts must
base its relief on some clear "indication of a significant causal
connection between the conduct enjoined or mandated and
the violation found directed toward the remedial goal intended." 3 Phillip E. Areeda & Herbert Hovenkamp, Antitrust
Law p 653(b), at 91-92 (1996). In a case such as the one
before us where sweeping equitable relief is employed to
remedy multiple violations, and some--indeed most--of the
findings of remediable violations do not withstand appellate
scrutiny, it is necessary to vacate the remedy decree since the
implicit findings of causal connection no longer exist to warrant our deferential affirmance.

     In short, we must vacate the remedies decree in its entirety
and remand the case for a new determination. This court has
drastically altered the District Court's conclusions on liability.
On remand, the District Court, after affording the parties a
proper opportunity to be heard, can fashion an appropriate
remedy for Microsoft's antitrust violations. In particular, the
court should consider which of the decree's conduct restrictions remain viable in light of our modification of the original
liability decision. While the task of drafting the remedies
decree is for the District Court in the first instance, because

of the unusually convoluted nature of the proceedings thus far, and a desire to advance the ultimate resolution of this important controversy, we offer some further guidance for the exercise of that discretion.

F.   On Remand

As a general matter, a district court is afforded broad discretion to enter that relief it calculates will best remedy the conduct it has found to be unlawful. See, e.g., Woerner v. United States Small Bus. Admin., 934 F.2d 1277, 1279 (D.C. Cir. 1991) (recognizing that an appellate court reviews a trial court's decision whether or not to grant equitable relief only for an abuse of discretion). This is no less true in antitrust cases. See, e.g., Ford Motor Co., 405 U.S. at 573 ("The District Court is clothed with 'large discretion' to fit the decree to the special needs of the individual case."); Md. & Va. Milk Producers Ass'n, Inc. v. United States, 362 U.S. 458, 473 (1960) ("The formulation of decrees is largely left to the discretion of the trial court...."). And divestiture is a common form of relief in successful antitrust prosecutions: it is indeed "the most important of antitrust remedies." See, e.g., United States v. E.I. du Pont de Nemours & Co., 366 U.S. 316, 331 (1961).

On remand, the District Court must reconsider whether the use of the structural remedy of divestiture is appropriate with respect to Microsoft, which argues that it is a unitary company. By and large, cases upon which plaintiffs rely in arguing for the split of Microsoft have involved the dissolution of entities formed by mergers and acquisitions. On the contrary, the Supreme Court has clarified that divestiture "has traditionally been the remedy for Sherman Act violations whose heart is intercorporate combination and control," du Pont, 366 U.S. at 329 (emphasis added), and that "[c]omplete divestiture is particularly appropriate where asset or stock acquisitions violate the antitrust laws," Ford Motor Co., 405 U.S. at 573 (emphasis added).

One apparent reason why courts have not ordered the dissolution of unitary companies is logistical difficulty. As the court explained in United States v. ALCOA, 91 F. Supp.

333, 416 (S.D.N.Y. 1950), a "corporation, designed to operate effectively as a single entity, cannot readily be dismembered of parts of its various operations without a marked loss of efficiency." A corporation that has expanded by acquiring its competitors often has preexisting internal lines of division along which it may more easily be split than a corporation that has expanded from natural growth. Although time and corporate modifications and developments may eventually fade those lines, at least the identifiable entities preexisted to create a template for such division as the court might later decree. With reference to those corporations that are not acquired by merger and acquisition, Judge Wyzanski accurately opined in United Shoe:

> United conducts all machine manufacture at one plant in Beverly, with one set of jigs and tools, one foundry, one laboratory for machinery problems, one managerial staff, and one labor force. It takes no Solomon to see that this organism cannot be cut into three equal and viable parts.

United States v. United Shoe Machine Co., 110 F. Supp. 295, 348 (D. Mass. 1953).

Depending upon the evidence, the District Court may find in a remedies proceeding that it would be no easier to split Microsoft in two than United Shoe in three. Microsoft's Offer of Proof in response to the court's denial of an evidentiary hearing included proffered testimony from its President and CEO Steve Ballmer that the company "is, and always has been, a unified company without free-standing business units. Microsoft is not the result of mergers or acquisitions." Microsoft further offered evidence that it is "not organized along product lines," but rather is housed in a single corporate headquarters and that it has

> only one sales and marketing organization which is responsible for selling all of the company's products, one basic research organization, one product support organization, one operations department, one information technology department, one facilities department, one purchasing department, one human resources department,

        one finance department, one legal department and one
        public relations department.

Defendant's Offer of Proof at 23-26, reprinted in 4 J.A. at
2764-67. If indeed Microsoft is a unitary company, division
might very well require Microsoft to reproduce each of these
departments in each new entity rather than simply allocate
the differing departments among them.

        In devising an appropriate remedy, the District Court also
should consider whether plaintiffs have established a sufficient causal connection between Microsoft's anticompetitive
conduct and its dominant position in the OS market. "Mere
existence of an exclusionary act does not itself justify full
feasible relief against the monopolist to create maximum
competition." 3 Areeda & Hovenkamp, Antitrust Law p 650a,
at 67. Rather, structural relief, which is "designed to eliminate the monopoly altogether ... require[s] a clearer indication of a significant causal connection between the conduct
and creation or maintenance of the market power." Id.
p 653b, at 91-92 (emphasis added). Absent such causation,
the antitrust defendant's unlawful behavior should be remed-
ied by "an injunction against continuation of that conduct."
Id. p 650a, at 67.

        As noted above, see supra Section II.C, we have found a
causal connection between Microsoft's exclusionary conduct
and its continuing position in the operating systems market
only through inference. See 3 Areeda & Hovenkamp, Antitrust Law p 653(b), at 91-92 (suggesting that "more extensive
equitable relief, particularly remedies such as divestiture
designed to eliminate the monopoly altogether, ... require a
clearer indication of significant causal connection between the
conduct and creation or maintenance of the market power").
Indeed, the District Court expressly did not adopt the position that Microsoft would have lost its position in the OS
market but for its anticompetitive behavior. Findings of
Fact p 411 ("There is insufficient evidence to find that, absent
Microsoft's actions, Navigator and Java already would have
ignited genuine competition in the market for Intel-
compatible PC operating systems."). If the court on remand
is unconvinced of the causal connection between Microsoft's

exclusionary conduct and the company's position in the OS market, it may well conclude that divestiture is not an appropriate remedy.

While we do not undertake to dictate to the District Court the precise form that relief should take on remand, we note again that it should be tailored to fit the wrong creating the occasion for the remedy.

G. Conclusion

In sum, we vacate the District Court's remedies decree for three reasons. First, the District Court failed to hold an evidentiary hearing despite the presence of remedies-specific factual disputes. Second, the court did not provide adequate reasons for its decreed remedies. Finally, we have drastically altered the scope of Microsoft's liability, and it is for the District Court in the first instance to determine the propriety of a specific remedy for the limited ground of liability which we have upheld.

VI. Judicial Misconduct

Canon 3A(6) of the Code of Conduct for United States Judges requires federal judges to "avoid public comment on the merits of [ ] pending or impending" cases. Canon 2 tells judges to "avoid impropriety and the appearance of impropriety in all activities," on the bench and off. Canon 3A(4) forbids judges to initiate or consider ex parte communications on the merits of pending or impending proceedings. Section 455(a) of the Judicial Code requires judges to recuse themselves when their "impartiality might reasonably be questioned." 28 U.S.C. s 455(a).

All indications are that the District Judge violated each of these ethical precepts by talking about the case with reporters. The violations were deliberate, repeated, egregious, and flagrant. The only serious question is what consequences should follow. Microsoft urges us to disqualify the District Judge, vacate the judgment in its entirety and toss out the findings of fact, and remand for a new trial before a different District Judge. At the other extreme, plaintiffs ask us to do nothing. We agree with neither position.

A.   The District Judge's Communications with the Press

Immediately after the District Judge entered final judgment on June 7, 2000, accounts of interviews with him began appearing in the press. Some of the interviews were held after he entered final judgment. See Peter Spiegel, Microsoft Judge Defends Post-trial Comments, Fin. Times (London), Oct. 7, 2000, at 4; John R. Wilke, For Antitrust Judge, Trust, or Lack of It, Really Was the Issue--In an Interview, Jackson Says Microsoft Did the Damage to Its Credibility in Court, Wall St. J., June 8, 2000, at A1. The District Judge also aired his views about the case to larger audiences, giving speeches at a college and at an antitrust seminar. See James V. Grimaldi, Microsoft Judge Says Ruling at Risk; Every Trial Decision Called 'Vulnerable', Wash. Post, Sept. 29, 2000, at E1; Alison Schmauch, Microsoft Judge Shares Experiences, The Dartmouth Online, Oct. 3, 2000.

From the published accounts, it is apparent that the Judge also had been giving secret interviews to select reporters before entering final judgment--in some instances long before. The earliest interviews we know of began in September 1999, shortly after the parties finished presenting evidence but two months before the court issued its Findings of Fact. See Joel Brinkley & Steve Lohr, U.S. vs. Microsoft: Pursuing a Giant; Retracing the Missteps in the Microsoft Defense, N.Y. Times, June 9, 2000, at A1. Interviews with reporters from the New York Times and Ken Auletta, another reporter who later wrote a book on the Microsoft case, continued throughout late 1999 and the first half of 2000, during which time the Judge issued his Findings of Fact, Conclusions of Law, and Final Judgment. See id.; Ken Auletta, Final Offer, The New Yorker, Jan. 15, 2001, at 40. The Judge "embargoed" these interviews; that is, he insisted that the fact and content of the interviews remain secret until he issued the Final Judgment.

Before we recount the statements attributed to the District Judge, we need to say a few words about the state of the

record. All we have are the published accounts and what the
reporters say the Judge said. Those accounts were not
admitted in evidence. They may be hearsay. See Fed. R.
Evid. 801(c); Metro. Council of NAACP Branches v. FCC, 46
F.3d 1154, 1165 (D.C. Cir. 1995) ("We seriously question
whether a New York Times article is admissible evidence of
the truthfulness of its contents.").

    We are of course concerned about granting a request to
disqualify a federal judge when the material supporting it has
not been admitted in evidence. Disqualification is never
taken lightly. In the wrong hands, a disqualification motion
is a procedural weapon to harass opponents and delay proceedings. If supported only by rumor, speculation, or innu-
endo, it is also a means to tarnish the reputation of a federal
judge.

    But the circumstances of this case are most unusual. By
placing an embargo on the interviews, the District Judge
ensured that the full extent of his actions would not be
revealed until this case was on appeal. Plaintiffs, in defend-
ing the judgment, do not dispute the statements attributed to
him in the press; they do not request an evidentiary hearing;
and they do not argue that Microsoft should have filed a
motion in the District Court before raising the matter on
appeal. At oral argument, plaintiffs all but conceded that the
Judge violated ethical restrictions by discussing the case in
public: "On behalf of the governments, I have no brief to
defend the District Judge's decision to discuss this case
publicly while it was pending on appeal, and I have no brief to
defend the judge's decision to discuss the case with reporters
while the trial was proceeding, even given the embargo on
any reporting concerning those conversations until after the
trial." 02/27/01 Ct. Appeals Tr. at 326.

    We must consider too that the federal disqualification
provisions reflect a strong federal policy to preserve the
actual and apparent impartiality of the federal judiciary.
Judicial misconduct may implicate that policy regardless of
the means by which it is disclosed to the public. Cf. The
Washington Post v. Robinson, 935 F.2d 282, 291 (D.C. Cir.

1991) (taking judicial notice of newspaper articles to ascertain whether a fact was within public knowledge). Also, in our analysis of the arguments presented by the parties, the specifics of particular conversations are less important than their cumulative effect.

For these reasons we have decided to adjudicate Microsoft's disqualification request notwithstanding the state of the record. The same reasons also warrant a departure from our usual practice of declining to address issues raised for the first time on appeal: the "matter of what questions may be taken up and resolved for the first time on appeal is one left primarily to the discretion of the courts of appeals, to be exercised on the facts of individual cases." Singleton v. Wulff, 428 U.S. 106, 121 (1976); accord Hormel v. Helvering, 312 U.S. 552, 556-57 (1941); Nat'l Ass'n of Mfrs. v. Dep't of Labor, 159 F.3d 597, 605-06 (D.C. Cir. 1998). We will assume the truth of the press accounts and not send the case back for an evidentiary hearing on this subject. We reach no judgment on whether the details of the interviews were accurately recounted.

The published accounts indicate that the District Judge discussed numerous topics relating to the case. Among them was his distaste for the defense of technological integration-- one of the central issues in the lawsuit. In September 1999, two months before his Findings of Fact and six months before his Conclusions of Law, and in remarks that were kept secret until after the Final Judgment, the Judge told reporters from the New York Times that he questioned Microsoft's integration of a web browser into Windows. Stating that he was "not a fan of integration," he drew an analogy to a 35-millimeter camera with an integrated light meter that in his view should also be offered separately: "You like the convenience of having a light meter built in, integrated, so all you have to do is press a button to get a reading. But do you think camera makers should also serve photographers who want to use a separate light meter, so they can hold it up, move it around?" Joel Brinkley & Steve Lohr, U.S. v. Microsoft 263 (2001). In other remarks, the Judge commented on the integration at the heart of the case: "[I]t was

quite clear to me that the motive of Microsoft in bundling the
Internet browser was not one of consumer convenience. The
evidence that this was done for the consumer was not credi-
ble.... The evidence was so compelling that there was an
ulterior motive." Wilke, Wall St. J. As for tying law in
general, he criticized this court's ruling in the consent decree
case, saying it "was wrongheaded on several counts" and
would exempt the software industry from the antitrust laws.
Brinkley & Lohr, U.S. v. Microsoft 78, 295; Brinkley &
Lohr, N.Y. Times.

     Reports of the interviews have the District Judge describ-
ing Microsoft's conduct, with particular emphasis on what he
regarded as the company's prevarication, hubris, and impeni-
tence. In some of his secret meetings with reporters, the
Judge offered his contemporaneous impressions of testimony.
He permitted at least one reporter to see an entry concerning
Bill Gates in his "oversized green notebook." Ken Auletta,
World War 3.0, at 112 (2001). He also provided numerous
after-the-fact credibility assessments. He told reporters that
Bill Gates' "testimony is inherently without credibility" and
"[i]f you can't believe this guy, who else can you believe?"
Brinkley & Lohr, U.S. v. Microsoft 278; Brinkley & Lohr,
N.Y. Times; see also Auletta, The New Yorker, at 40. As for
the company's other witnesses, the Judge is reported as
saying that there "were times when I became impatient with
Microsoft witnesses who were giving speeches." "[T]hey
were telling me things I just flatly could not credit." Brinkley & Lohr, N.Y. Times. In an interview given the day he
entered the break-up order, he summed things up: "Falsus in
uno, falsus in omnibus": "Untrue in one thing, untrue in
everything." "I don't subscribe to that as absolutely true.
But it does lead one to suspicion. It's a universal human
experience. If someone lies to you once, how much else can
you credit as the truth?" Wilke, Wall St. J.

     According to reporter Auletta, the District Judge told him
in private that, "I thought they [Microsoft and its executives]
didn't think they were regarded as adult members of the
community. I thought they would learn." Auletta, World
War 3.0, at 14. The Judge told a college audience that "Bill

Gates is an ingenious engineer, but I don't think he is that
adept at business ethics. He has not yet come to realise
things he did (when Microsoft was smaller) he should not
have done when he became a monopoly." Spiegel, Fin. Times.
Characterizing Gates' and his company's "crime" as hubris,
the Judge stated that "[i]f I were able to propose a remedy of
my devising, I'd require Mr. Gates to write a book report" on
Napoleon Bonaparte, "[b]ecause I think [Gates] has a Napole-
onic concept of himself and his company, an arrogance that
derives from power and unalloyed success, with no leavening
hard experience, no reverses." Auletta, The New Yorker, at
41; see also Auletta, World War 3.0, at 397. The Judge
apparently became, in Auletta's words, "increasingly troubled
by what he learned about Bill Gates and couldn't get out of
his mind the group picture he had seen of Bill Gates and Paul
Allen and their shaggy-haired first employees at Microsoft."
The reporter wrote that the Judge said he saw in the picture
"a smart-mouthed young kid who has extraordinary ability
and needs a little discipline. I've often said to colleagues that
Gates would be better off if he had finished Harvard."
Auletta, World War 3.0, at 168-69; see also Auletta, The
New Yorker, at 46 (reporting the District Judge's statement
that "they [Microsoft and its executives] don't act like grown-
ups!" "[T]o this day they continue to deny they did anything
wrong.").

    The District Judge likened Microsoft's writing of incrimina-
ting documents to drug traffickers who "never figure out that
they shouldn't be saying certain things on the phone."
Brinkley & Lohr, U.S. v. Microsoft 6; Brinkley & Lohr,
N.Y. Times. He invoked the drug trafficker analogy again to
denounce Microsoft's protestations of innocence, this time
with a reference to the notorious Newton Street Crew that
terrorized parts of Washington, D.C. Reporter Auletta wrote
in The New Yorker that the Judge

        went as far as to compare the company's declaration of
        innocence to the protestations of gangland killers. He
        was referring to five gang members in a racketeering,
        drug-dealing, and murder trial that he had presided over

four years earlier. In that case, the three victims had
had their heads bound with duct tape before they were
riddled with bullets from semi-automatic weapons. "On
the day of the sentencing, the gang members maintained
that they had done nothing wrong, saying that the whole
case was a conspiracy by the white power structure to
destroy them," Jackson recalled. "I am now under no
illusions that miscreants will realize that other parts of
society will view them that way."

Auletta, The New Yorker, at 40-41; Auletta, World War 3.0,
at 369-70 (same); see also Auletta, The New Yorker, at 46.

     The District Judge also secretly divulged to reporters his
views on the remedy for Microsoft's antitrust violations. On
the question whether Microsoft was entitled to any process at
the remedy stage, the Judge told reporters in May 2000 that
he was "not aware of any case authority that says I have to
give them any due process at all. The case is over. They
lost." Brinkley & Lohr, N.Y. Times. Another reporter has
the Judge asking "[w]ere the Japanese allowed to propose
terms of their surrender?" Spiegel, Fin. Times. The District
Judge also told reporters the month before he issued his
break-up order that "[a]ssuming, as I think they are, [ ] the
Justice Department and the states are genuinely concerned
about the public interest," "I know they have carefully stud-
ied all the possible options. This isn't a bunch of amateurs.
They have consulted with some of the best minds in America
over a long period of time." "I am not in a position to
duplicate that and re-engineer their work. There's no way I
can equip myself to do a better job than they have done."
Brinkley & Lohr, N.Y. Times; cf. Final Judgment, at 62-63.

     In February 2000, four months before his final order
splitting the company in two, the District Judge reportedly
told New York Times reporters that he was "not at all
comfortable with restructuring the company," because he was
unsure whether he was "competent to do that." Brinkley &
Lohr, N.Y. Times; see also Brinkley & Lohr, U.S. v. Microsoft 277-78 (same); cf. Auletta, World War 3.0, at 370
(comment by the Judge in April 2000 that he was inclining

toward behavioral rather than structural remedies). A few
months later, he had a change of heart. He told the same
reporters that "with what looks like Microsoft intransigence,
a breakup is inevitable." Brinkley & Lohr, N.Y. Times; see
also Brinkley & Lohr, U.S. v. Microsoft 315. The Judge
recited a "North Carolina mule trainer" story to explain his
change in thinking from "[i]f it ain't broken, don't try to fix it"
and "I just don't think that [restructuring the company] is
something I want to try to do on my own" to ordering
Microsoft broken in two:

> He had a trained mule who could do all kinds of wonder-
> ful tricks. One day somebody asked him: "How do you
> do it? How do you train the mule to do all these
> amazing things?" "Well," he answered, "I'll show you."
> He took a 2-by-4 and whopped him upside the head.
> The mule was reeling and fell to his knees, and the
> trainer said: "You just have to get his attention."

Brinkley & Lohr, U.S. v. Microsoft 278. The Judge added:
"I hope I've got Microsoft's attention." Id.; see also Grimaldi, Wash. Post (comments by the Judge blaming the break-up
on Microsoft's intransigence and on what he perceived to be
Microsoft's responsibility for the failure of settlement talks);
Spiegel, Fin. Times (the Judge blaming break-up on Microsoft's intransigence).

B.   Violations of the Code of Conduct for United States
      Judges

     The Code of Conduct for United States Judges was
adopted by the Judicial Conference of the United States in
1973. It prescribes ethical norms for federal judges as a
means to preserve the actual and apparent integrity of the
federal judiciary. Every federal judge receives a copy of the
Code, the Commentary to the Code, the Advisory Opinions of
the Judicial Conference's Committee on Codes of Conduct,
and digests of the Committee's informal, unpublished opinions. See II Guide to Judiciary Policies and Procedures
(1973). The material is periodically updated. Judges who
have questions about whether their conduct would be consis-

tent with the Code may write to the Codes of Conduct
Committee for a written, confidential opinion. See Introduction, Code of Conduct. The Committee traditionally responds promptly. A judge may also seek informal advice
from the Committee's circuit representative.

      While some of the Code's Canons frequently generate
questions about their application, others are straightforward
and easily understood. Canon 3A(6) is an example of the
latter. In forbidding federal judges to comment publicly "on
the merits of a pending or impending action," Canon 3A(6)
applies to cases pending before any court, state or federal,
trial or appellate. See Jeffrey M. Shaman et al., Judicial
Conduct and Ethics s 10.34, at 353 (3d ed. 2000). As "impending" indicates, the prohibition begins even before a case
enters the court system, when there is reason to believe a
case may be filed. Cf. E. Wayne Thode, Reporter's Notes to
Code of Judicial Conduct 54 (1973). An action remains
"pending" until "completion of the appellate process." Code
of Conduct Canon 3A(6) cmt.; Comm. on Codes of Conduct,
Adv. Op. No. 55 (1998).

      The Microsoft case was "pending" during every one of the
District Judge's meetings with reporters; the case is "pending" now; and even after our decision issues, it will remain
pending for some time. The District Judge breached his
ethical duty under Canon 3A(6) each time he spoke to a
reporter about the merits of the case. Although the reporters interviewed him in private, his comments were public.
Court was not in session and his discussion of the case took
place outside the presence of the parties. He provided his
views not to court personnel assisting him in the case, but to
members of the public. And these were not just any members of the public. Because he was talking to reporters, the
Judge knew his comments would eventually receive widespread dissemination.

      It is clear that the District Judge was not discussing purely
procedural matters, which are a permissible subject of public
comment under one of the Canon's three narrowly drawn
exceptions. He disclosed his views on the factual and legal

matters at the heart of the case. His opinions about the
credibility of witnesses, the validity of legal theories, the
culpability of the defendant, the choice of remedy, and so
forth all dealt with the merits of the action. It is no excuse
that the Judge may have intended to "educate" the public
about the case or to rebut "public misperceptions" purportedly caused by the parties. See Grimaldi, Wash. Post; Microsoft Judge Says He May Step down from Case on Appeal,
Wall St. J., Oct. 30, 2000. If those were his intentions, he
could have addressed the factual and legal issues as he saw
them--and thought the public should see them--in his Findings of Fact, Conclusions of Law, Final Judgment, or in a
written opinion. Or he could have held his tongue until all
appeals were concluded.

    Far from mitigating his conduct, the District Judge's insis-
tence on secrecy--his embargo--made matters worse. Concealment of the interviews suggests knowledge of their impropriety. Concealment also prevented the parties from nipping
his improprieties in the bud. Without any knowledge of the
interviews, neither the plaintiffs nor the defendant had a
chance to object or to seek the Judge's removal before he
issued his Final Judgment.

    Other federal judges have been disqualified for making
limited public comments about cases pending before them.
See In re Boston's Children First, 244 F.3d 164 (1st Cir.
2001); In re IBM Corp., 45 F.3d 641 (2d Cir. 1995); United
States v. Cooley, 1 F.3d 985 (10th Cir. 1993). Given the
extent of the Judge's transgressions in this case, we have
little doubt that if the parties had discovered his secret
liaisons with the press, he would have been disqualified,
voluntarily or by court order. Cf. In re Barry, 946 F.2d 913
(D.C. Cir. 1991) (per curiam); id. at 915 (Edwards, J., dissenting).

    In addition to violating the rule prohibiting public com-
ment, the District Judge's reported conduct raises serious
questions under Canon 3A(4). That Canon states that a
"judge should accord to every person who is legally interested
in a proceeding, or the person's lawyer, full right to be heard

according to law, and, except as authorized by law, neither initiate nor consider ex parte communications on the merits, or procedures affecting the merits, of a pending or impending proceeding." Code of Conduct Canon 3A(4).

What did the reporters convey to the District Judge during their secret sessions? By one account, the Judge spent a total of ten hours giving taped interviews to one reporter. Auletta, World War 3.0, at 14 n.*. We do not know whether he spent even more time in untaped conversations with the same reporter, nor do we know how much time he spent with others. But we think it safe to assume that these interviews were not monologues. Interviews often become conversations. When reporters pose questions or make assertions, they may be furnishing information, information that may reflect their personal views of the case. The published accounts indicate this happened on at least one occasion. Ken Auletta reported, for example, that he told the Judge "that Microsoft employees professed shock that he thought they had violated the law and behaved unethically," at which time the Judge became "agitated" by "Microsoft's 'obstinacy'." Id. at 369. It is clear that Auletta had views of the case. As he wrote in a Washington Post editorial, "[a]nyone who sat in [the District Judge's] courtroom during the trial had seen ample evidence of Microsoft's sometimes thuggish tactics." Ken Auletta, Maligning the Microsoft Judge, Wash. Post, Mar. 7, 2001, at A23.

The District Judge's repeated violations of Canons 3A(6) and 3A(4) also violated Canon 2, which provides that "a judge should avoid impropriety and the appearance of impropriety in all activities." Code of Conduct Canon 2; see also In re Charge of Judicial Misconduct, 47 F.3d 399, 400 (10th Cir. Jud. Council 1995) ("The allegations of extra-judicial comments cause the Council substantial concern under both Canon 3A(6) and Canon 2 of the Judicial Code of Conduct."). Canon 2A requires federal judges to "respect and comply with the law" and to "act at all times in a manner that promotes public confidence in the integrity and impartiality of the judiciary." Code of Conduct Canon 2A. The Code of Conduct is the law with respect to the ethical obligations of federal judges, and it is clear the District Judge violated it on multiple occasions in this case. The rampant disregard for the judiciary's ethical obligations that the public witnessed in this case undoubtedly jeopardizes "public confidence in the integrity" of the District Court proceedings.

Another point needs to be stressed. Rulings in this case have potentially huge financial consequences for one of the nation's largest publicly-traded companies and its investors. The District Judge's secret interviews during the trial provided a select few with inside information about the case, information that enabled them and anyone they shared it with to anticipate rulings before the Judge announced them to the world. Although he "embargoed" his comments, the Judge had no way of policing the reporters. For all he knew there may have been trading on the basis of the information he secretly conveyed. The public cannot be expected to maintain confidence in the integrity and impartiality of the federal judiciary in the face of such conduct.

C.   Appearance of Partiality

The Code of Conduct contains no enforcement mechanism. See Thode, Reporter's Notes to Code of Judicial Conduct 43. The Canons, including the one that requires a judge to disqualify himself in certain circumstances, see Code of Conduct Canon 3C, are self-enforcing. There are, however, remedies extrinsic to the Code. One is an internal disciplinary proceeding, begun with the filing of a complaint with the clerk of the court of appeals pursuant to 28 U.S.C. s 372(c). Another is disqualification of the offending judge under either 28 U.S.C. s 144, which requires the filing of an affidavit while the case is in the District Court, or 28 U.S.C. s 455, which does not. Microsoft urges the District Judge's disqualification under s 455(a): a judge "shall disqualify himself in any proceeding in which his impartiality might reasonably be questioned." 28 U.S.C. s 455(a). The standard for disqualification under s 455(a) is an objective one. The question is whether a reasonable and informed observer would question the judge's impartiality. See In re Barry, 946 F.2d at 914;

see also In re Aguinda, 241 F.3d 194, 201 (2d Cir. 2001);
Richard E. Flamm, Judicial Disqualification s 24.2.1 (1996).

"The very purpose of s 455(a) is to promote confidence in
the judiciary by avoiding even the appearance of impropriety
whenever possible." Liljeberg v. Health Servs. Acquisition
Corp., 486 U.S. 847, 865 (1988). As such, violations of the
Code of Conduct may give rise to a violation of s 455(a) if
doubt is cast on the integrity of the judicial process. It has
been argued that any "public comment by a judge concerning
the facts, applicable law, or merits of a case that is sub judice
in his court or any comment concerning the parties or their
attorneys would raise grave doubts about the judge's objectiv-
ity and his willingness to reserve judgment until the close of
the proceeding." William G. Ross, Extrajudicial Speech:
Charting the Boundaries of Propriety, 2 Geo. J. Legal Ethics
589, 598 (1989). Some courts of appeals have taken a hard
line on public comments, finding violations of s 455(a) for
judicial commentary on pending cases that seems mild in
comparison to what we are confronting in this case. See
Boston's Children First, 244 F.3d 164 (granting writ of
mandamus ordering district judge to recuse herself under
s 455(a) because of public comments on class certification and
standing in a pending case); In re IBM Corp., 45 F.3d 641
(granting writ of mandamus ordering district judge to recuse
himself based in part on the appearance of partiality caused
by his giving newspaper interviews); Cooley, 1 F.3d 985
(vacating convictions and disqualifying district judge for appearance of partiality because he appeared on television
program Nightline and stated that abortion protestors in a
case before him were breaking the law and that his injunction
would be obeyed).

While s 455(a) is concerned with actual and apparent impropriety, the statute requires disqualification only when a
judge's "impartiality might reasonably be questioned." 28
U.S.C. s 455(a). Although this court has condemned public
judicial comments on pending cases, we have not gone so far
as to hold that every violation of Canon 3A(6) or every
impropriety under the Code of Conduct inevitably destroys
the appearance of impartiality and thus violates s 455(a).

See In re Barry, 946 F.2d at 914; see also Boston's Children
First, 244 F.3d at 168; United States v. Fortier, 242 F.3d
1224, 1229 (10th Cir. 2001).

     In this case, however, we believe the line has been crossed.
The public comments were not only improper, but also would
lead a reasonable, informed observer to question the District
Judge's impartiality. Public confidence in the integrity and
impartiality of the judiciary is seriously jeopardized when
judges secretly share their thoughts about the merits of
pending cases with the press. Judges who covet publicity, or
convey the appearance that they do, lead any objective observer to wonder whether their judgments are being influenced by the prospect of favorable coverage in the media.
Discreet and limited public comments may not compromise a
judge's apparent impartiality, but we have little doubt that
the District Judge's conduct had that effect. Appearance
may be all there is, but that is enough to invoke the Canons
and s 455(a).

     Judge Learned Hand spoke of "this America of ours where
the passion for publicity is a disease, and where swarms of
foolish, tawdry moths dash with rapture into its consuming
fire...." Learned Hand, The Spirit of Liberty 132-33 (2d
ed. 1953). Judges are obligated to resist this passion. In-
dulging it compromises what Edmund Burke justly regarded
as the "cold neutrality of an impartial judge." Cold or not,
federal judges must maintain the appearance of impartiality.
What was true two centuries ago is true today: "Deference to
the judgments and rulings of courts depends upon public
confidence in the integrity and independence of judges."
Code of Conduct Canon 1 cmt. Public confidence in judicial
impartiality cannot survive if judges, in disregard of their
ethical obligations, pander to the press.

     We recognize that it would be extraordinary to disqualify a
judge for bias or appearance of partiality when his remarks
arguably reflected what he learned, or what he thought he
learned, during the proceedings. See Liteky v. United States,
510 U.S. 540, 554-55 (1994); United States v. Barry, 961 F.2d
260, 263 (D.C. Cir. 1992). But this "extrajudicial source" rule

has no bearing on the case before us. The problem here is
not just what the District Judge said, but to whom he said it
and when. His crude characterizations of Microsoft, his
frequent denigrations of Bill Gates, his mule trainer analogy
as a reason for his remedy--all of these remarks and others
might not have given rise to a violation of the Canons or of
s 455(a) had he uttered them from the bench. See Liteky,
510 U.S. at 555-56; Code of Conduct Canon 3A(6) (exception
to prohibition on public comments for "statements made in
the course of the judge's official duties"). But then Microsoft
would have had an opportunity to object, perhaps even to
persuade, and the Judge would have made a record for review
on appeal. It is an altogether different matter when the
statements are made outside the courtroom, in private meetings unknown to the parties, in anticipation that ultimately
the Judge's remarks would be reported. Rather than mani-
festing neutrality and impartiality, the reports of the interviews with the District Judge convey the impression of a
judge posturing for posterity, trying to please the reporters
with colorful analogies and observations bound to wind up in
the stories they write. Members of the public may reasonably question whether the District Judge's desire for press
coverage influenced his judgments, indeed whether a
publicity-seeking judge might consciously or subconsciously
seek the publicity-maximizing outcome. We believe, therefore, that the District Judge's interviews with reporters created an appearance that he was not acting impartially, as the
Code of Conduct and s 455(a) require.

D.   Remedies for Judicial Misconduct and Appearance of
      Partiality

      1. Disqualification

      Disqualification is mandatory for conduct that calls a
judge's impartiality into question. See 28 U.S.C. s 455(a); In
re School Asbestos Litig., 977 F.2d 764, 783 (3d Cir. 1992).
Section 455 does not prescribe the scope of disqualification.
Rather, Congress "delegated to the judiciary the task of
fashioning the remedies that will best serve the purpose" of
the disqualification statute. Liljeberg, 486 U.S. at 862.

At a minimum, s 455(a) requires prospective disqualification of the offending judge, that is, disqualification from the judge's hearing any further proceedings in the case. See United States v. Microsoft Corp., 56 F.3d 1448, 1463-65 (D.C. Cir. 1995) (per curiam) ("Microsoft I"). Microsoft urges retroactive disqualification of the District Judge, which would entail disqualification antedated to an earlier part of the proceedings and vacatur of all subsequent acts. Cf. In re School Asbestos Litig., 977 F.2d at 786 (discussing remedy options).

"There need not be a draconian remedy for every violation of s 455(a)." Liljeberg, 486 U.S. at 862. Liljeberg held that a district judge could be disqualified under s 455(a) after entering final judgment in a case, even though the judge was not (but should have been) aware of the grounds for disqualification before final judgment. The Court identified three factors relevant to the question whether vacatur is appropriate: "in determining whether a judgment should be vacated for a violation of s 455(a), it is appropriate to consider the risk of injustice to the parties in the particular case, the risk that the denial of relief will produce injustice in other cases, and the risk of undermining the public's confidence in the judicial process." Id. at 864. Although the Court was discussing s 455(a) in a slightly different context (the judgment there had become final after appeal and the movant sought to have it vacated under Rule 60(b)), we believe the test it propounded applies as well to cases such as this in which the full extent of the disqualifying circumstances came to light only while the appeal was pending. See In re School Asbestos Litig., 977 F.2d at 785.

Our application of Liljeberg leads us to conclude that the appropriate remedy for the violations of s 455(a) is disqualification of the District Judge retroactive only to the date he entered the order breaking up Microsoft. We therefore will vacate that order in its entirety and remand this case to a different District Judge, but will not set aside the existing Findings of Fact or Conclusions of Law (except insofar as specific findings are clearly erroneous or legal conclusions are incorrect).

This partially retroactive disqualification minimizes the risk of injustice to the parties and the damage to public confidence in the judicial process. Although the violations of the Code of Conduct and s 455(a) were serious, full retroactive disqualification is unnecessary. It would unduly penalize plaintiffs, who were innocent and unaware of the misconduct, and would have only slight marginal deterrent effect.

Most important, full retroactive disqualification is unnecessary to protect Microsoft's right to an impartial adjudication. The District Judge's conduct destroyed the appearance of impartiality. Microsoft neither alleged nor demonstrated that it rose to the level of actual bias or prejudice. There is no reason to presume that everything the District Judge did is suspect. See In re Allied-Signal Inc., 891 F.2d 974, 975-76 (1st Cir. 1989); cf. Liberty Lobby, Inc. v. Dow Jones & Co., 838 F.2d 1287, 1301-02 (D.C. Cir. 1988). Although Microsoft challenged very few of the findings as clearly erroneous, we have carefully reviewed the entire record and discern no basis to suppose that actual bias infected his factual findings.

The most serious judicial misconduct occurred near or during the remedial stage. It is therefore commensurate that our remedy focus on that stage of the case. The District Judge's impatience with what he viewed as intransigence on the part of the company; his refusal to allow an evidentiary hearing; his analogizing Microsoft to Japan at the end of World War II; his story about the mule--all of these out-of-court remarks and others, plus the Judge's evident efforts to please the press, would give a reasonable, informed observer cause to question his impartiality in ordering the company split in two.

To repeat, we disqualify the District Judge retroactive only to the imposition of the remedy, and thus vacate the remedy order for the reasons given in Section V and because of the appearance of partiality created by the District Judge's misconduct.

2. Review of Findings of Fact and Conclusions of
Law

   Given the limited scope of our disqualification of the District Judge, we have let stand for review his Findings of Fact
and Conclusions of Law. The severity of the District Judge's
misconduct and the appearance of partiality it created have
led us to consider whether we can and should subject his
factfindings to greater scrutiny. For a number of reasons we
have rejected any such approach.

   The Federal Rules require that district court findings of
fact not be set aside unless they are clearly erroneous. See
Fed. R. Civ. P. 52(a). Ordinarily, there is no basis for
doubting that the District Court's factual findings are entitled
to the substantial deference the clearly erroneous standard
entails. But of course this is no ordinary case. Deference to
a district court's factfindings presumes impartiality on the
lower court's part. When impartiality is called into question,
how much deference is due?

   The question implies that there is some middle ground, but
we believe there is none. As the rules are written, district
court factfindings receive either full deference under the
clearly erroneous standard or they must be vacated. There is
no de novo appellate review of factfindings and no intermedi-
ate level between de novo and clear error, not even for
findings the court of appeals may consider sub-par. See
Amadeo v. Zant, 486 U.S. 214, 228 (1988) ("The District
Court's lack of precision, however, is no excuse for the Court
of Appeals to ignore the dictates of Rule 52(a) and engage in
impermissible appellate factfinding."); Anderson v. City of
Bessemer City, 470 U.S. 564, 571-75 (1985) (criticizing district
court practice of adopting a party's proposed factfindings but
overturning court of appeals' application of "close scrutiny" to
such findings).

   Rule 52(a) mandates clearly erroneous review of all district
court factfindings: "Findings of fact, whether based on oral
or documentary evidence, shall not be set aside unless clearly
erroneous, and due regard shall be given to the opportunity
of the trial court to judge of the credibility of the witnesses."
Fed. R. Civ. P. 52(a). The rule "does not make exceptions or
purport to exclude certain categories of factual findings from

the obligation of a court of appeals to accept a district court's
findings unless clearly erroneous." Pullman-Standard v.
Swint, 456 U.S. 273, 287 (1982); see also Anderson, 470 U.S.
at 574-75; Inwood Labs., Inc. v. Ives Labs., Inc., 456 U.S.
844, 855-58 (1982). The Supreme Court has emphasized on
multiple occasions that "[i]n applying the clearly erroneous
standard to the findings of a district court sitting without a
jury, appellate courts must constantly have in mind that their
function is not to decide factual issues de novo." Zenith
Radio Corp. v. Hazeltine Research, Inc., 395 U.S. 100, 123
(1969); Anderson, 470 U.S. at 573 (quoting Zenith).

   The mandatory nature of Rule 52(a) does not compel us to
accept factfindings that result from the District Court's mis-
application of governing law or that otherwise do not permit
meaningful appellate review. See Pullman-Standard, 456

U.S. at 292; Inwood Labs., 456 U.S. at 855 n.15. Nor must
we accept findings that are utterly deficient in other ways.
In such a case, we vacate and remand for further factfinding.
See 9 Moore's Federal Practice s 52.12[1] (Matthew Bender
3d ed. 2000); 9A Charles A. Wright & Arthur R. Miller,
Federal Practice and Procedure s 2577, at 514-22 (2d ed.
1995); cf. Icicle Seafoods, Inc. v. Worthington, 475 U.S. 709,
714 (1986); Pullman-Standard, 456 U.S. at 291-92.

    When there is fair room for argument that the District
Court's factfindings should be vacated in toto, the court of
appeals should be especially careful in determining that the
findings are worthy of the deference Rule 52(a) prescribes.
See, e.g., Thermo Electron Corp. v. Schiavone Constr. Co., 915
F.2d 770, 773 (1st Cir. 1990); cf. Bose Corp. v. Consumers
Union of United States, Inc., 466 U.S. 485, 499 (1984). Thus,
although Microsoft alleged only appearance of bias, not actual
bias, we have reviewed the record with painstaking care and
have discerned no evidence of actual bias. See S. Pac.
Communications Co. v. AT & T, 740 F.2d 980, 984 (D.C. Cir.
1984); Cooley, 1 F.3d at 996 (disqualifying district judge for

appearance of partiality but noting that "the record of the proceedings below ... discloses no bias").

In light of this conclusion, the District Judge's factual findings both warrant deference under the clear error standard of review and, though exceedingly sparing in citations to the record, permit meaningful appellate review. In reaching these conclusions, we have not ignored the District Judge's reported intention to craft his factfindings and Conclusions of Law to minimize the breadth of our review. The Judge reportedly told Ken Auletta that "[w]hat I want to do is confront the Court of Appeals with an established factual record which is a fait accompli." Auletta, World War 3.0, at 230. He explained: "part of the inspiration for doing that is that I take mild offense at their reversal of my preliminary injunction in the consent-decree case, where they went ahead and made up about ninety percent of the facts on their own." Id. Whether the District Judge takes offense, mild or severe, is beside the point. Appellate decisions command compliance, not agreement. We do not view the District Judge's remarks as anything other than his expression of disagreement with this court's decision, and his desire to provide extensive factual findings in this case, which he did.

VII. Conclusion

The judgment of the District Court is affirmed in part, reversed in part, and remanded in part. We vacate in full the Final Judgment embodying the remedial order, and remand the case to the District Court for reassignment to a different trial judge for further proceedings consistent with this opinion.